Sunset

Vegetable
Cook Book

**By the Editors of Sunset Books
and Sunset Magazine**

Lane Publishing Co. • Menlo Park, California

From Artichokes to Zucchini...

Today's abundant harvest of flavorful, high-quality produce finds its way into a grand diversity of dishes. Long underrated, vegetables are enjoying new popularity as creative cooks feature them throughout the meal—from appetizers and salads to entrées, breads, and desserts.

Enjoy this book of vegetables—it's a cornucopia of imaginative suggestions for savoring your old favorites and discovering new ones. Here you'll find recipes suitable for virtually any occasion, from simple family dishes to more festive fare. Use the detailed charts as a handy guide to selecting, preparing, and cooking fresh vegetables. Be an adventurer—experiment with herbs and spices, and let the seasonal harvest determine the menu, for top quality and best value.

For their cooperation in sharing props for use in our photographs, we extend special thanks to The Best of All Worlds, Cotton Works, House of Today, Taylor & Ng, and Williams-Sonoma Kitchenware.

Supervising Editor: **Cornelia Fogle**

Research & Text: **Joan Griffiths**
Elizabeth Friedman

Design: **Lea Damiano Phelps**

Illustrations: **Jacqueline Osborn**

Photo Editor: **Lynne B. Morrall**

Photographers

Darrow M. Watt: 42, 50, 63, 67, 83, 86, 94.
Nikolay Zurek: 34, 39, 47, 55, 58, 70, 75, 78, 91.

Cover: Flaming red bell peppers make vibrant vessels for a hearty filling of Italian sausage, eggplant, tomato, and cheese. Garden-fresh herbs—thyme and fennel—add a special touch to Stuffed Bell Peppers Italiano (recipe on page 60). Photographed by Nikolay Zurek.

Editor, Sunset Books: David E. Clark

Second printing May 1984

Contents

*M*ore than ever before, fresh and flavorful vegetables are widely available, rushed from farm to market to reach consumers in peak condition.

Today's bountiful supply of high-quality produce gives you the opportunity to discover all kinds of dishes—from appetizers to entrées to desserts. If you love vegetables, want to learn more about them or discover new varieties, or just seek appealing ideas to enliven family and company meals, then this book is for you.

Introduction

Vegetables gain new popularity

Long overcooked and underrated, vegetables have attained new popularity. Gardeners enjoying a bountiful harvest look for new ways to use a surplus of zucchini, green beans, or tomatoes. Calorie and nutrition-conscious cooks, knowing that fresh produce is a rich natural source of fiber, vitamins, and minerals, plan menus including lots of vegetables.

Improved growing methods have extended the seasons of many vegetables, expanding market variety and availability. New and unfamiliar kinds of produce challenge innovative cooks to experiment with seasonings and preparation techniques. Travelers re-create at home the dishes they first enjoyed abroad. Family chefs want fresh ideas to pep up weekday menus.

How to use this book

You'll find more than recipes in this book. First, check the chart on pages 6–13; it will guide you in the selection, storage, and basic preparation of more than 50 vegetables, and suggest seasonings to complement the flavor of each one.

On pages 14 and 15, you'll learn cutting and chopping techniques designed to speed cooking time, release flavor, and display each vegetable attractively.

The charts beginning on page 16 give you explicit instructions for a variety of basic cooking methods. Look here for information on such familiar techniques as boiling and steaming; or read up on a different method—stir-frying or butter-steaming, for example—and then treat family or guests to a favorite vegetable cooked a new way.

Vegetables can play an important role in all parts of the meal, from appetizers and soups to breads and desserts. Imaginative recipes, created to enhance the natural flavors of fresh vegetables, begin on page 26. Selected with busy cooks in mind, many of these dishes are simple, requiring only brief cooking. (For the simplest preparation of all, present a colorful array of crisp raw vegetables with one of the lively dips on page 31.) Other dishes can be prepared ahead, ideal for easy entertaining.

Throughout the book, special features offer still more ideas—you'll find, among other things, tips on growing sprouts at home; ideas for seasoned butters, pickles, and relishes; and the very best recipes for sauces and dressings.

Let vegetables perk up your menus

Fresh vegetables add color and variety to every culinary occasion, from the simplest family meal to the most lavish dinner party. Let the available produce and the season be your guide. Select and enjoy the finest produce your market offers, and follow the seasonal harvest for best values and top quality.

As you expand your vegetable repertoire, you'll discover lively new combinations and introduce your family and friends to a wide variety of tempting and unusual vegetable dishes. Bon appétit!

FRESH VEGETABLES ABOUND in a lush array of harvest bounty: kale, asparagus, okra, radishes (red and daikon), beets, fennel, tomato, napa cabbage, basil, cherry tomatoes, green onions.

Vegetables A to Z ...The Basics

Though many vegetables are available beyond their natural growing seasons, the choicest and most flavorful vegetables are those grown and harvested in season. Home-grown or local vegetables are the best—luscious red tomatoes from your own back yard, corn on the cob purchased at a farmer's roadside stand. And top quality isn't the only advantage of buying vegetables at the peak of their season; prices are lowest then, too.

Whether you buy your produce at a large supermarket or at a small greengrocery, take time to choose the best vegetables your store offers. Sift through the

VEGETABLE SELECTION & MONTHS OF PEAK AVAILABILITY	AMOUNT (4 servings)	STORAGE
ARTICHOKES. Choose artichokes with tight, compact heads that feel heavy for their size. Surface brown spots (from frost) are harmless and indicate a meaty artichoke. Size is not an indication of quality. *March through May*	4 medium to large (2¾ to 4-inch diameter)	Place unwashed artichokes in a plastic bag and refrigerate for up to 1 week.
ASPARAGUS. Select firm, brittle spears that are bright green almost the entire length, with tightly closed tips. *March through June*	1½ to 2 pounds	Wrap ends in a damp paper towel. Place unwashed asparagus in a plastic bag and refrigerate for up to 4 days.
BEANS, GREEN, ITALIAN, WAX. Choose small crisp beans that are bright and blemish-free. *July through September*	1 pound	Place unwashed beans in a plastic bag and refrigerate for up to 4 days.
BEANS, SHELLED—cranberry, fava, lima. Look for thick, broad, tightly closed pods that are bulging with large beans. If purchased shelled, beans should look plump and fresh. **Cranberry**—*August through October;* **fava**—*April through June;* **lima**—*July through September*	2½ to 3 pounds unshelled or 1 pound shelled	Place unwashed pods or shelled beans in a plastic bag and refrigerate for up to 4 days.
BEET GREENS—See **GREENS**		
BEETS. Select small to medium beets that are firm and have smooth skins. Leaves should be deep green and fresh-looking. *June through October*	1½ to 2 pounds	Cut off tops, leaving 1 to 2 inches of stem attached to crown. Do not trim roots. Reserve tops and cook separately (see **GREENS**). Place unwashed beets in a plastic bag; refrigerate for up to 1 week.
BELGIAN ENDIVE. Look for crisp, 4 to 6-inch-long heads that are creamy white tinged with light yellow at the tips. *September through May*	6 to 8 heads	Place unwashed endive in a plastic bag and refrigerate for up to 4 days.
BOK CHOY. Choose heads with bright white stalks and shiny dark leaves. Avoid heads with slippery brown spots on leaves; this indicates overchilling, which robs vegetable of flavor. *All year*	1¼ to 1½ pounds (1 small to medium head)	Place unwashed bok choy in a plastic bag and refrigerate for up to 4 days.
BROCCOLI. Look for compact clusters of tightly closed dark green flowerets. Avoid heads with yellowing flowerets and thick, woody stems. *All year*	1 to 1½ pounds	Place unwashed broccoli in a plastic bag and refrigerate for up to 5 days.
BRUSSELS SPROUTS. Choose small, firm Brussels sprouts that are compact and feel heavy for their size. They should be bright green and free of blemishes. *August through April*	1¼ to 1½ pounds	Pull off and discard any limp or discolored leaves. Place unwashed sprouts in a plastic bag and refrigerate for up to 3 days.
CABBAGE, GREEN, RED, SAVOY. Choose firm heads that feel heavy for their size. Outer leaves should look fresh, have good color, and be free of blemishes. *All year*	1 to 1½ pounds (1 small to medium head)	Place unwashed cabbage in a plastic bag and refrigerate for up to 1 week.
CABBAGE, NAPA (also called celery cabbage, Chinese cabbage). Look for fresh, crisp leaves free of blemishes. *All year*	About 1½ pounds (1 medium-size head)	Place unwashed cabbage in a plastic bag and refrigerate for up to 4 days.
CARROTS. Select firm carrots that are smooth, well shaped, and brightly colored. Any tops should look fresh and be bright green. *All year*	1 pound (1 medium-size bunch)	Cut off and discard tops, leaving 1 to 2 inches attached to carrot. Place unwashed carrots in a plastic bag and refrigerate for up to two weeks.
CAULIFLOWER. Choose firm, compact, creamy white heads pressed tightly together. A yellow tinge and spreading flowerets indicate overmaturity. Any leaves should be crisp and bright green. *All year*	1¼ to 1½ pounds (1 medium-size head)	Place unwashed cauliflower in a plastic bag and refrigerate for up to 1 week.

mounds of oversize, tough green beans to find the thin, tender ones; avoid limp, tired celery, choosing instead the freshest, crispest bunch. A few moments spent in selecting superior produce can help transform an ordinary meal into a special occasion.

Some vegetables retain their peak flavor and texture longer than others. Root vegetables, such as carrots, potatoes, and onions, can be stored successfully for many weeks. In contrast, asparagus, corn on the cob, and leaf lettuce are among the most perishable.

In the following chart, you'll find tips for selecting the best produce and storing it to maintain peak condition. The chart also suggests appropriate cooking methods and seasonings for each vegetable. For detailed information on each of the suggested cooking methods, see pages 16–25. And for descriptions of the cutting and chopping techniques mentioned in the chart, turn to pages 14–15.

BASIC PREPARATION	SUGGESTED COOKING METHODS	SUGGESTED SEASONINGS
Prepare just before cooking. With a stainless steel knife, slice off stem. Remove and discard coarse outer leaves and cut off top third of artichoke. With kitchen shears, trim thorny tips of remaining leaves. Rinse well and plunge immediately into acidulated water (3 tablespoons vinegar or lemon juice per quart water).	Boil, steam, microwave	Melted butter, garlic butter (page 65) mayonnaise, hollandaise sauce (page 77)
Snap off and discard tough ends. If desired, peel stalks with a vegetable peeler to remove scales. Plunge into a large quantity of cold water; lift out and drain. Leave spears whole or cut into slices.	Boil, steam, microwave, stir-fry, butter-steam, grill	Butter, tarragon, lemon juice, hollandaise sauce (page 77)
Rinse beans; snap off and discard ends. Leave small beans whole; cut larger beans into crosswise or diagonal slices, or into long French-style slivers.	Boil, steam, microwave, stir-fry, butter-steam, grill	Butter, chives, dill weed, thyme, crumbled bacon
Remove beans from pods and rinse.	Boil	Butter, savory, lemon juice
Scrub well, but do not peel (to preserve their rich color, beets are usually cooked in their jackets). Leave roots, stems, and skin intact during cooking to prevent "bleeding." After cooking, let cool; then trim root and stem, and slip off skins under cold running water.	Boil, microwave, butter-steam, bake	Butter, mustard butter, chives, dill weed, thyme, lemon juice, grated orange peel, dash of wine vinegar
Pull off and discard any wilted or discolored outer leaves and trim stem ends. Rinse under cold running water. To use in salads, separate individual leaves or slice crosswise. To cook, leave whole or cut in half lengthwise.	Boil	Butter, minced parsley, lemon juice, grated lemon peel, chopped toasted nuts
Plunge into a large quantity of cold water; lift out and drain. Cut leaves from stems (leaves cook faster). Slice stems crosswise and coarsely shred leaves.	Boil, steam, microwave, stir-fry, butter-steam	Butter, ginger, soy sauce
Rinse; cut off and discard base of stalks, leaving about 3½ inches of stalks. Peel bottom few inches of stalks, if desired. Cut lengthwise into spears. Leave whole and slash through bottom inch of stalks; or slice stalks crosswise, leaving flowerets whole.	Boil, steam, microwave, stir-fry, butter-steam	Butter, dill weed, rosemary, lemon juice
Trim stem ends and rinse. To ensure even cooking, cut a shallow "X" into end of each stem.	Boil, steam, microwave, butter-steam	Butter, basil, chives, dill weed, minced parsley, rosemary, thyme
Pull off and discard any wilted outer leaves. Rinse, cut in half lengthwise, and cut out core. Cut into wedges or shred.	Boil, steam, microwave, stir-fry, butter-steam	Butter, caraway seeds, dill weed
Pull off and discard any wilted outer leaves; rinse. Cut off base, cut in half lengthwise, then slice crosswise.	Microwave, stir-fry, butter-steam	Butter, ginger, soy sauce
Trim top and root ends. Scrub well; if desired, peel with a vegetable peeler and rinse. Cook whole; or slice, dice, shred, or cut into julienne strips.	Boil, steam, microwave, stir-fry, butter-steam, bake, grill	Butter, basil, chives, dill weed, ginger, mint, nutmeg, minced parsley, lemon juice, brown sugar
Remove and discard outer leaves and cut out core; rinse. Leave head whole or break into flowerets.	Boil, steam, microwave, stir-fry, butter-steam	Butter, chives, dill weed, nutmeg, minced parsley, lemon juice, mornay sauce, hollandaise sauce (page 77)

(Continued on next page)

VEGETABLE SELECTION & MONTHS OF PEAK AVAILABILITY	AMOUNT (4 servings)	STORAGE
CELERY AND CELERY HEARTS. Look for rigid, crisp, green stalks with fresh-looking leaves. Avoid celery with limp or rubbery stalks. *All year*	1½ pounds (1 medium-size bunch or 2 hearts)	Rinse and shake dry. Place in a plastic bag and refrigerate for up to 2 weeks.
CELERY ROOT (also called celeriac, celery knob). Select small to medium roots that are firm and relatively clean. Any tops should look fresh and be bright green. *October through April*	1 to 1½ pounds (3 small or 2 medium-size roots)	Place unwashed roots in a plastic bag and refrigerate for up to 1 week.
CHAYOTE. Choose firm young chayotes that are free of blemishes. Color is not an indication of quality—chayotes range from pale to medium green. *October through March*	1½ to 2 pounds (2 medium to large)	Store chayotes, unwrapped, in a cool (50°), dry, dark place with good ventilation for up to 1 month. Or place chayotes in a plastic bag and refrigerate for up to 1 week.
CHICORY (also called curly endive). Look for fresh, crisp, tender heads with deep green outer leaves free of blemishes. *August through December*	1 pound (1 large head)	Rinse under cold running water, then shake off excess. Dry greens. Wrap in a dry cloth or paper towel, place in a plastic bag, and refrigerate for up to 2 days.
COLLARDS—See **GREENS**		
CORN. It's best to buy and cook corn on the day it's picked. Look for fresh ears with green husks, moist stems, and silk ends that are free of decay and worm injury. When pierced with thumbnail, kernels should give a spurt of thin, milky juice. Thick liquid and tough skin indicate overmaturity. *May through September*	4 large or 8 small to medium ears (2 ears yield about 1 cup kernels)	Place unhusked ears in a plastic bag and refrigerate for up to 2 days.
CUCUMBERS—**Armenian, English or European, lemon, marketer** (most common variety), **pickling.** Choose firm dark green **marketer** and **pickling** cucumbers that are well shaped and slender. Soft, yellowing cucumbers are overmature. Select long, firm examples of pale green **Armenian** and straight **English** or **European** (hothouse) cucumbers. Pale yellow green **lemon** cucumbers should be small (2 to 3-inch diameter). **Armenian, lemon**—*July through October;* **English** or **European, marketer** (most common variety)—*All year;* **pickling**—*July through September*	1 medium-size **Armenian** or **English**; 2 small or 1 medium to large **marketer**	**Marketers** are waxed to prevent moisture loss and can be refrigerated whole, unwrapped, for up to 1 week; if cut, wrap in plastic wrap. Wrap other varieties, whole or cut-up, in plastic wrap and refrigerate; **lemon** cucumbers for up to 5 days; others for up to 1 week.
DANDELION GREENS—See **GREENS**		
EGGPLANT. Look for firm, heavy, shiny, deep purple eggplants with bright green stems. Dull color and rust-colored spots are signs of old age. *July through October*	1¼ to 1½ pounds (1 large or 2 small to medium)	Place unwashed eggplant in a plastic bag and refrigerate for up to 5 days.
ESCAROLE (also called broad-leafed endive). Look for fresh, crisp, tender heads with deep green outer leaves and pale inner ones. *August through December*	1 pound (1 large head)	Rinse under cold running water, pulling back outer leaves to expose gritty center; shake off excess water. Dry greens. Wrap in a dry cloth or paper towel, place in a plastic bag, and refrigerate for up to 2 days.
FENNEL (also called anise, finocchio). Look for firm, white bulbs with rigid, crisp stalks and feathery bright green leaves. *October through April*	3 pounds (3 or 4 medium-size bulbs, each 3 to 4-inch diameter)	Place unwashed fennel in a plastic bag and refrigerate for up to 1 week.
GARLIC. Choose firm, dry bulbs with tightly closed cloves and smooth skins. Avoid bulbs with sprouting green shoots. *All year*	1 large head	Store unwrapped garlic in a cool (50°), dry, dark place with good ventilation for 2 to 3 months.
GREENS—**beet, collards, dandelion, kale, mustard, turnip.** Look for fresh, tender leaves that are deep green and free of blemishes. Avoid bunches with thick, coarse-veined leaves. **Beet**— *June through October;* **collards, dandelion, kale, mustard**—*January through April;* **turnip**—*October through March*	1½ to 2 pounds	Remove and discard damaged, yellowed, or wilted leaves. Rinse well under cold running water; shake off excess. Dry greens. Wrap in a dry cloth or paper towel and place in a plastic bag. Refrigerate **beet** and **turnip** greens for up to 2 days, **collards, dandelion, kale,** and **mustard** greens for up to 4 days.
HERBS. Look for herbs with allover green color. Yellowing leaves indicate herbs are old; black, watery areas indicate bruising. **Cilantro (fresh coriander), parsley**—*All year;* **basil, chervil, chives, dill weed, marjoram, mint, oregano, rosemary, sage, savory, tarragon, thyme**—*July through September*		Rinse under cold running water; shake off excess water. Wrap in a dry cloth or paper towel, place in a plastic bag, and refrigerate for up to 4 days (parsley for up to 1 week).

BASIC PREPARATION	SUGGESTED COOKING METHODS	SUGGESTED SEASONINGS
Separate stalks and rinse thoroughly. Trim off leaves (reserve for soups and stock) and base; cut out brown spots. To remove strings from outer stalks, pull strings with a knife from top of stalk down to base; discard. Dice stalks; or cut into slices or julienne strips. Rinse hearts and cut in half lengthwise.	Boil, steam, stir-fry, butter-steam	Butter, tarragon, thyme
Scrub with a vegetable brush, and cut off and discard top and root ends. Peel away thick outer skin with a sturdy knife. Cut out spots where vegetable is pitted. Slice, dice, shred, or cut into julienne strips. To keep peeled or cut surfaces of raw celery root white, submerge immediately in a bowl of acidulated water (3 tablespoons vinegar or lemon juice per quart water).	Boil, butter-steam	Butter, dill weed, tarragon
Rinse well. Cut in half lengthwise. Or peel and slice crosswise or quarter lengthwise through seed (cooked seed is edible).	Boil, steam, butter-steam	Butter, basil, oregano, nutmeg, thyme, lemon juice, lime juice, orange juice
Separate leaves; leave whole or tear into bite-size pieces.	Best served raw	Salad dressings (page 53)
Remove and discard husk and silk; trim stem end. To cut corn from cob, stand cooked or raw ear on end and slice straight down, leaving kernel bases attached to cob. If desired, scrape cob with back of a knife to remove remaining corn pulp and "milk".	Boil, steam, microwave, bake, grill	Butter, chili powder, oregano, lime juice
Rinse; if desired, peel with a vegetable peeler or score lengthwise with tines of a fork. To seed, cut cucumber in half lengthwise and scoop out seeds with a spoon. To use in salads or sandwiches, slice whole cucumbers crosswise; to butter-steam, peel, seed, and slice.	Butter-steam **Armenian, English, marketer;** do not cook **lemon** or **pickling** cucumbers	Butter, chervil, chives, dill weed, minced parsley
Rinse and pat dry. Cut off and discard stem end; peel, if desired. Cut into cubes or ½-inch-thick slices.	Bake	Garlic butter (page 65), basil, marjoram, oregano, minced parsley, thyme
Tear leaves into bite-size pieces.	Best served raw	Salad dressings (page 53)
Rinse thoroughly. Trim stalks to within ¾ to 1 inch of bulb. Discard hard outside stalks and bulb base; reserve leaves for seasoning cooked bulb. Cut bulb lengthwise into halves or quarters, or dice, or cut into julienne strips.	Boil, steam, stir-fry, butter-steam	Butter, fennel leaves, dash of whipping cream
To use as a seasoning, break into cloves. To peel, cut off root end of clove, crush clove with side of a knife blade, and pull skin away. Mince or press through a garlic press. To bake, leave unpeeled heads whole.	Bake	Needs no seasoning
Tear out and discard tough center ribs. Use leaves whole, or cut or tear into bite-size pieces.	Boil **collards, kale, mustard, turnip;** microwave **kale, mustard;** butter-steam **beet, turnip; dandelion** best served raw	Butter, oregano, lemon juice, dash of wine vinegar, crumbled bacon
Pull or cut off leaves, and chop or mince. Use as a seasoning or garnish.		

(Continued on next page)

Vegetables A to Z ... The Basics

VEGETABLE SELECTION & MONTHS OF PEAK AVAILABILITY	AMOUNT (4 servings)	STORAGE
JICAMA. Choose firm, well-formed jicama that are free of blemishes. *October through June*	1 pound	Store whole unwashed jicama at room temperature for 2 to 3 weeks. Wrap cut pieces in plastic wrap and refrigerate for up to 1 week.
KALE—See **GREENS**		
KOHLRABI. Choose small, tender bulbs with fresh, green leaves, avoid those with scars and blemishes. *June through October*	4 small to medium bulbs	Cut off tops; reserve for other uses, if desired. Place unwashed kohlrabi in a plastic bag and refrigerate for up to 1 week.
LEEKS. Select leeks with clean, white bottoms and fresh-looking, crisp, green tops. *October through May*	1½ pounds (about 1 bunch)	Place unwashed leeks in a plastic bag and refrigerate for up to 1 week.
LETTUCE—bibb, Boston, butter, iceberg, red or green leaf, **limestone, romaine.** Choose heads of **iceberg** with fresh, green outer leaves; heads should give a little under pressure. Good **romaine** has crisp, deep green outer leaves without brown spots or decay. **Bibb, Boston, butter, red or green leaf,** and **limestone** lettuce should have tender, fresh-looking leaves free of tip burn and bruising. *All year*	1 small to medium head **iceberg** or **romaine;** 1 to 2 heads **butter;** or 1 large head **leaf**	Rinse before storing. To rinse **iceberg,** hold head, core side down, under cold running water; drain. Rinse **romaine, butter,** and **leaf** lettuce under running water, separating individual leaves. Dry well. Wrap in dry cloth or paper towel and place in a plastic bag; refrigerate **iceberg** and **romaine** for up to 5 days, **butter** and **leaf** lettuce for up to 2 days.
MUSHROOMS. Select smooth, plump mushrooms with caps closed around stems; avoid spotted mushrooms and those that have open caps with dark gills exposed. *All year*	1 pound	Place unwashed mushrooms in a paper bag and refrigerate for up to 4 days. If desired, place a damp paper towel inside bag to help mushrooms retain moisture.
MUSTARD GREENS—See **GREENS**		
OKRA (also called gumbo). Select small to medium pods that are deep green and firm. Pods should be free of blemishes and flexible enough to bend easily. *July through October*	1 pound	Place unwashed okra in a plastic bag and refrigerate for up to 3 days.
ONIONS, DRY—boiling, mild red, shallots, mild white, **yellow.** Choose firm, dry onions with characteristically brittle outer skin. Avoid those with sprouting green shoots and dark spots. *All year*	1 pound	Store whole onions, unwrapped, in a cool (50°) dry, dark place with good ventilation for up to 2 months. Wrap cut pieces in plastic wrap and refrigerate for up to 4 days.
ONIONS, GREEN (also called scallions). Choose green onions with crisp, bright green tops and clean, white bottoms. *All year*		Place unwashed onions in a plastic bag and refrigerate for up to 1 week.
PARSNIPS. Choose small to medium parsnips that are firm, smooth, well shaped. Avoid large woody parsnips. *November through March*	1 pound	Place unwashed parsnips in a plastic bag and refrigerate for up to 10 days.
PEAS, EDIBLE-POD—**Chinese pea pods (also called snow or sugar peas), sugar snap peas.** Look for firm, crisp, bright green pods. *February through June*	1 pound	Place unwashed pods in a plastic bag and refrigerate for up to 3 days.
PEAS, GREEN (also called shell peas). Select small, plump, bright green pods that are firm, crisp, and well filled with medium-size peas. *April through August*	2 to 2½ pounds unshelled (1 lb. unshelled yields about 1 cup shelled)	Place unwashed pods in plastic bag and refrigerate for up to 3 days.
PEPPERS, GREEN OR RED BELL. Select bright, glossy peppers that are firm, well shaped, and thick walled; avoid those with soft spots and gashes. When allowed to ripen on the bush, green peppers turn brilliant red. *July through September*	3 or 4 medium to large	Place unwashed peppers in a plastic bag and refrigerate; **green peppers** for up to 5 days, **red peppers** for up to 3 days.
POTATOES, RUSSET. Choose firm potatoes with reasonably smooth skins; avoid those with sprouting eyes, soft black spots, and green areas. *All year*	4 medium to large	Store potatoes, unwrapped, in a cool (50°), dry, dark place with good ventilation for up to 2 months or at room temperature for up to 1 week.
POTATOES, SWEET (and "yams"). Choose sweet potatoes that are firm and well shaped with bright, uniformly colored skin. Two types are available: the one usually called **sweet potato** has light yellow flesh and a dry, mealy consistency when cooked; the second type, usually called **yams** in the market, has orange flesh and is sweet and moist after cooking. *October through March*	4 medium to large	Store sweet potatoes, unwrapped, in a cool (50°), dry, dark place with good ventilation for up to 2 months or at room temperature for up to 1 week.

BASIC PREPARATION	SUGGESTED COOKING METHODS	SUGGESTED SEASONINGS
Scrub well and peel. Slice, dice, or cut into julienne strips for salads or to use in combination stir-fry dishes.	Stir-fry	Lemon or lime juice, soy sauce
Scrub young bulbs. Peel mature bulbs to remove tough outer skin. Use whole, slice, or dice.	Boil, butter-steam	Butter, chives, dill weed, lemon juice, dash of wine vinegar
Cut off and discard root ends. Trim tops, leaving about 1½ inches of dark green leaves. Strip away and discard coarse outer leaves, leaving tender inner ones. Cut leeks in half lengthwise. Hold each half under cold running water, separating layers to rinse out dirt.	Boil, steam, microwave, stir-fry, butter-steam	Butter, chervil, minced parsley, tarragon, crumbled bacon
Tear leaves into bite-size pieces for salads. If desired, cut out core and shred **iceberg.**	Butter-steam **iceberg**	Salad dressings (page 53)
To clean, wipe with a damp cloth or mushroom brush, or rinse briefly under cold running water; pat dry. Trim stem base. Use whole, slice lengthwise through stem, or chop.	Microwave, stir-fry, butter-steam	Butter, minced parsley, tarragon, thyme, dash of dry sherry
For long, slow cooking, trim stem ends, then rinse and slice okra; pods contain a milky liquid that will help thicken stews and gumbos. *For more quickly cooked dishes,* leave pods whole to contain liquid, since it can give okra an unpleasant, sticky texture. Rinse pods and trim stem ends carefully to avoid piercing pods.	Boil, steam	Butter, chives, minced parsley, lemon juice
Trim stem and root ends from **red, white, and yellow onions** and **shallots;** peel outer skin. Leave whole, quarter, slice, or chop. To peel small **boiling onions,** pour boiling water over onions, let stand for 2 to 3 minutes, then drain. Trim stem and root ends; peel and discard outer skin. Cut a shallow "X" into each stem end to ensure even cooking and keep onion intact.	Microwave, stir-fry, butter-steam, bake, **mild red, mild white, yellow;** boil, steam, microwave **boiling onions**	Butter, minced parsley, thyme, brown or granulated sugar
Rinse and pat dry. Trim root ends; strip off and discard wilted outer leaves. Trim brown or dried areas from tops. Slice or cut into julienne strips for salads or to use in combination stir-fry dishes.	Stir-fry	Salad dressings (page 53), ginger, soy sauce
Trim tops and root ends. Peel with a vegetable peeler and rinse. Leave whole, dice, slice, or cut into sticks or julienne strips.	Boil, steam, microwave, stir-fry, butter-steam, bake	Butter, basil, tarragon, thyme, lemon juice, brown sugar
Break off both ends; remove and discard strings. Rinse.	Boil, steam, microwave, stir-fry, butter-steam	Butter, soy sauce
Remove peas from pods and rinse.	Boil, steam, microwave, stir-fry, butter-steam, grill	Butter, basil, chervil, chives, mint, nutmeg, minced parsley, rosemary, tarragon, thyme
Rinse; remove stem, seeds, and pith. Leave whole, cut in half lengthwise, slice, dice, or cut into julienne strips.	Stir-fry, butter-steam, bake	Basil, oregano, dash of wine vinegar
Scrub well and dry. To bake, pierce and leave whole. To keep peeled or sliced potatoes white, submerge in a bowl of cold water immediately after cutting.	Microwave, bake, grill	Butter, chives, paprika, minced parsley, crumbled bacon, sour cream
Scrub well and dry. To bake, pierce and leave whole.	Boil, steam, microwave, bake	Butter, lemon or orange juice, grated lemon or orange peel, brown sugar

(Continued on next page)

Vegetables A to Z ... The Basics **11**

VEGETABLE SELECTION & MONTHS OF PEAK AVAILABILITY	AMOUNT (4 servings)	STORAGE
POTATOES, THIN-SKINNED (red and white "new" potatoes). Look for firm, well-shaped potatoes with reasonably smooth skins; avoid those with sprouting eyes and yellow spots. *All year*	1½ pounds (6 to 8 small)	Store potatoes, unwrapped, in a cool (50°), dry, dark place with good ventilation for up to 1 month. Store unwrapped at room temperature or in the refrigerator for up to 1 week.
PUMPKIN—See **SQUASH, WINTER**		
RADISHES, DAIKON. Choose firm, white, small to medium daikon, 1 to 1½ inches in diameter. *All year*	1 large (about 1 pound)	Place unwashed daikon in a plastic bag and refrigerate for up to 10 days.
RADISHES, RED. Look for smooth, crisp, firm radishes that are well formed and have good red color. Bright green tops indicate freshness. *All year*	1 to 1½ bunches	Place unwashed radishes in a plastic bag and refrigerate for up to 1 week.
RUTABAGAS. Choose small to medium rutabagas that are smooth and firm and feel heavy for their size. Lightweight rutabagas may be woody. *October through March*	1½ to 2 pounds	Store rutabagas, unwrapped, in a cool, (50°), dry, dark place with good ventilation for up to 2 months. Store unwrapped at room temperature or in the refrigerator for up to 1 week.
SHALLOTS—See **ONIONS, DRY**		
SORREL. Select young, fresh looking leaves that are free of blemishes. *July through October*	1 pound (about 10 cups leaves)	Wrap unwashed sorrel in a cloth or paper towel, place in a plastic bag, and refrigerate for up to 2 days.
SPINACH. Choose bunches having crisp, tender, deep green leaves, with few yellow leaves or blemishes. *All year*	1½ pounds (about 2 bunches)	Discard yellow, damaged, and wilted leaves. Remove and discard tough stems and midribs. Plunge into a large quantity of cold water; lift out and drain. For salads, dry well. Wrap in a dry cloth or paper towel, place in a plastic bag, and refrigerate for up to 3 days. To cook, do not dry; cook in water that clings to leaves.
SPROUTS, BEAN AND ALFALFA. Select small, tender examples of both varieties. Bean sprouts should be crisp and white with beans attached. *All year*	1 pound bean sprouts	Place unwashed sprouts in a plastic bag and refrigerate for up to 4 days.
SQUASH, SPAGHETTI. Squash should have hard, thick shell and feel heavy for its size. *August through February*	2 pounds	Store whole squash, unwrapped, at room temperature for up to 2 months.
SQUASH, SUMMER—crookneck, pattypan, zucchini. Select firm, small to medium squash with smooth, glossy, tender skin. Squash should feel heavy for their size. *June through September*	1 to 1½ pounds	Place unwashed squash in a plastic bag and refrigerate for up to 5 days.
SQUASH, WINTER—acorn, banana, butternut, Hubbard, pumpkin. Choose squash that have hard, thick shells and feel heavy for their size. Flesh should be thick and bright yellow-orange. *September through March*	1½ to 2 pounds	Store whole squash, unwrapped, in a cool, (50°), dry, dark place with good ventilation for up to 2 months. Wrap cut pieces in plastic wrap and refrigerate for up to 5 days.
SUNCHOKES (also called Jerusalem artichokes). Choose tubers that are firm and free of mold. *October through April*	1 to 1½ pounds	Place unwashed tubers in a plastic bag and refrigerate for up to 1 week.
SWISS CHARD. Look for bunches with fresh glossy, dark green leaves and heavy white or red stems. *July through October*	1½ to 2 pounds	Place unwashed chard in a plastic bag and refrigerate for up to 3 days.
TOMATOES. Choose tomatoes that are smooth, well formed, and firm but not hard. Color varies according to variety and ripeness. Tomatoes that are picked ripe are richly colored; those picked before ripening are paler in color. *July through September*	1 to 1½ pounds (4 medium-size)	Store unwashed tomatoes at room temperature, stem end down, until slightly soft. Refrigerate very ripe tomatoes, unwrapped, for up to 4 days.
TURNIP GREENS—See **GREENS**		
TURNIPS. Choose firm, small to medium turnips (2 to 3-inch diameter) that have smooth skin and feel heavy for their size. If they have tops, leaves should be bright green and tender. *October through March*	1½ to 2 pounds (about 4 medium-size)	Remove tops; if desired, cook tops separately (see **GREENS**). Place unwashed turnips in a plastic bag and refrigerate for up to 1 week.
WATERCRESS. Select vivid green leaves; avoid wilted and yellowed leaves. *All year*	1 medium to large bunch or 2 small bunches	Rinse under cold running water. Stand stems in a container of cold water; then cover tops with a plastic bag. Refrigerate for up to 2 days.
YAMS—See **POTATOES, SWEET**		

BASIC PREPARATION	SUGGESTED COOKING METHODS	SUGGESTED SEASONINGS
Scrub well and dry. Boil, steam, or pierce and bake small **red potatoes** whole; cut larger, long **white potatoes** into quarters before cooking. To keep peeled or sliced potatoes white, submerge in a bowl of cold water immediately after cutting.	Boil, steam, bake, grill	Butter, caraway seeds, dill weed, minced parsley, rosemary, crumbled bacon
Rinse, trim stem and root ends, and peel. Slice or shred to use in salads, soups, or combination stir-fry dishes.	Stir-fry	Dash of white rice vinegar, soy sauce
Rinse well; cut off and discard tops and roots. Use whole; or slice, shred, or quarter.		Salad dressings (page 53)
Rinse and peel with a vegetable peeler. Leave whole; or quarter, slice, dice, or cut into julienne strips.	Boil, steam, stir-fry, butter-steam, bake	Butter, caraway seeds, cinnamon, dill weed, lemon juice, brown sugar
Remove and discard stems and midribs. Plunge into a large quantity of cold water; lift out and drain. To reduce color loss and acidity, blanch leaves before cooking. Or serve raw in salads.		Sliced green onion, crumbled bacon
Keep leaves whole, tear into bite-size pieces, or shred.	Boil, steam, microwave, stir-fry, butter-steam	Butter, basil, mint, nutmeg, oregano, grated lemon peel, crumbled bacon
Rinse **bean sprouts;** discard discolored ones. Drain. Rinse and drain **alfalfa sprouts;** use raw in salads, sandwiches, or other dishes.	Microwave, stir-fry, butter-steam **bean sprouts;** do not cook **alfalfa sprouts**	Butter, ginger, soy sauce **(bean sprouts)**
Rinse; do not peel. To bake, pierce shell in several places; leave whole. To microwave, cut in half lengthwise and remove seeds.	Microwave, bake	Butter, basil, oregano, minced parsley
Trim ends and rinse. Do not peel. Leave whole, dice, or cut into slices or julienne strips.	Boil, steam, microwave, stir-fry, butter-steam, grill	Butter, basil, oregano, minced parsley
Rinse. Cut **acorn** or **butternut** squash or **pumpkin** in half lengthwise; cut **banana** or **Hubbard** squash into serving-size pieces. Remove and discard seeds and fibers. Bake unpeeled; for other cooking methods, peel and cut into cubes, spears, or slices.	Boil, steam, bake **all varieties;** microwave **acorn, banana, butternut;** butter-steam **banana, Hubbard, pumpkin;** grill **banana, Hubbard**	Butter, allspice, cardamom, cinnamon, nutmeg, brown sugar
Scrub well or peel with a vegetable peeler. Submerge immediately in a bowl of acidulated water (3 tablespoons vinegar or lemon juice per quart water) to prevent discoloration. Leave whole; or slice or dice.	Boil, steam, butter-steam	Butter, tarragon, lemon juice
Plunge into a large quantity of cold water; lift out and drain. Cut leaves from stems (leaves cook faster). Slice stems crosswise and shred leaves.	Boil, steam, microwave, stir-fry, butter-steam	Butter, basil, nutmeg, oregano, crumbled bacon
To peel, submerge tomatoes in boiling water for 30 seconds to 1 minute, then plunge immediately into cold water; lift out and slip off skins. Or hold tomato on a fork over a flame until skin splits; then peel. To seed, slice in half crosswise and squeeze out seeds. Leave whole; or slice, chop, or cut into wedges.	Bake	Basil, chives, dill weed, oregano, minced parsley
Rinse. Bake whole turnips unpeeled; peel for other cooking methods. Leave whole; or dice, slice, or cut into quarters or julienne strips.	Boil, steam, microwave, stir-fry, butter-steam, bake	Butter, basil, caraway seeds, brown sugar, crumbled bacon
Remove tough stems. Use leaves and tender part of stems in salads or soups, tucked into sandwiches, or as a garnish.		Salad dressings (page 53)

Cutting & Chopping Fresh Vegetables

Some would argue that the advent of the food processor has made the chef's knife obsolete. We disagree. Though machines can slice, shred, and chop, mastering these techniques yourself will lead to faster results for small quantities. And such mastery is certainly more gratifying—with patience and practice, you'll find yourself producing julienne strips as deftly as a professional chef.

When chopping, dicing, slicing, or shredding, grip the vegetable firmly with your fingertips, keeping them curled back toward your palm. In this way you'll protect your fingers from the knife's edge.

When deciding which way to cut vegetables, keep in mind that small cuts—mince and dice—cook quickly; when they're cooked in combination, their flavors marry readily. Cuts exposing a large surface area, such as diagonal slice and julienne, also cook quickly. It's best to cook these two cuts over high heat—by stir-frying or butter-steaming, for example.

Shredding. To shred cabbage or head lettuce, cut head in half through core; then cut core out and discard it. Place head, cut side down, on board; cut crosswise into ⅛ to ¼-inch-thick slices. If desired, cut shreds crosswise into halves or thirds.

Diagonal slicing. This is a particularly attractive way to slice long vegetables. Slice crosswise, with the knife slanted at a 45° to 60° angle. Make cuts at regular intervals—from ¼ to 1½ inches apart, depending on the desired thickness of slices.

Chopping. To chop an onion, first trim ends and peel onion; then cut in half lengthwise through ends. Place onion, cut side down, on a board. Make a series of cuts parallel to the board and ⅛ to ¼ inch apart, cutting just to root end but not through it. Next make a series of cuts lengthwise from root to stem end and ⅛ to ¼ inch apart, cutting through to board. Finally, cut onion crosswise into ⅛ to ¼-inch-thick slices, starting at stem end.

To chop other vegetables, just follow the same principles. To chop celery, for example, make several lengthwise cuts, then cut stalk crosswise.

Mincing. Start with coarsely chopped herbs or vegetables. Grip the knife handle with one hand; steady the knife tip with your other hand. Use the tip as a pivot point as you move the heel of the knife up and down through the chopped vegetables, transcribing an arc with your grip hand. Push vegetables back into a pile; continue mincing until vegetables are cut as finely as you wish.

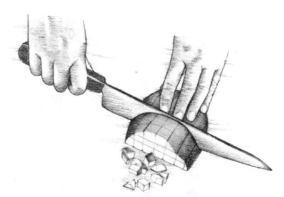

Cutting julienne strips. Julienne strips—matchstick pieces often used in salads and stir-fry dishes—can be cut from both long and round vegetables. First cut a thin slice from the bottom of the vegetable so it will lie flat; then cut lengthwise into ⅛-inch-thick slices. Stack slices half at a time, cut side down, and cut lengthwise again into ⅛-inch-thick sticks; then cut crosswise into 2-inch lengths.

Dicing and cubing. To dice or cube a long or round vegetable, first cut a thin slice from the bottom so vegetable will lie flat; or cut vegetable in half lengthwise through ends. Slice lengthwise, making cuts ⅛ to ¼ inch apart for dice, ½ to 1 inch apart for cubes. Stack slices half at a time, cut side down, and cut lengthwise again to form sticks; then push all sticks together and slice crosswise.

Boiling & Steaming Fresh Vegetables

Before boiling or steaming fresh vegetables, check the chart beginning on page 6 for tips on selection, storage, and basic preparation. Keep in mind that whole or cut-up vegetables cook more evenly if they're uniform in size and shape.

To boil vegetables. Bring designated amount of water to a boil over high heat; add vegetables. When water returns to a boil, cover pan if specified in chart, reduce heat to medium (water should boil throughout cooking time), and begin timing.

To steam vegetables. Cookware shops have various utensils for steaming, but the simplest and least expensive is a collapsible metal steaming basket, available in two sizes to fit into ordinary pans. If you have a metal colander and a pan big enough to hold it, that's another possibility. Whatever you use, it should accommodate whole vegetables such as potatoes in a single layer, or cut-up vegetables or small vegetables such as peas in an even layer no deeper than 1½ to 2 inches.

Place rack in pan; pour in water to a depth of 1 to 1½ inches (water should not touch bottom of rack). Bring to a boil over high heat; then place vegetables on rack. Cover pan, reduce heat to medium (water should boil throughout cooking time) and begin timing. If necessary, add boiling water to pan to maintain water level throughout cooking time.

To test for doneness. Cooking time depends on freshness and maturity of vegetables. Test after minimum cooking time; if necessary, continue to cook, testing frequently, until vegetables are done to your liking. Most cooked vegetables should be just tender when pierced; potatoes and beets should be tender throughout. Leafy vegetables should appear wilted and have bright color.

To serve. Immediately drain vegetables, if necessary, reserving any liquid to use in soups, stock, or sauces. To serve vegetables hot, season to taste with salt and pepper; or choose one or more of the seasonings suggested in the chart beginning on page 6. To serve vegetables cold, immediately plunge them into cold water; when cool, drain again.

VEGETABLE For amount for 4 servings, see chart on pages 6–13	Container	BOILING Amount of Water	Time	STEAMING Time	TEST FOR DONENESS
ARTICHOKES Whole (medium-size)	5 to 6-qt. kettle, covered	3–4 qts. plus 2 tablespoons vinegar	30–45 minutes	25–35 minutes	Stem end tender when pierced
ASPARAGUS Spears	Wide frying pan, covered	1 inch	7–10 minutes	8–12 minutes	Tender when pierced
Slices (½ to 1 inch)	Wide frying pan, covered	½ inch	2–5 minutes	5–7 minutes	Tender when pierced
BEANS, GREEN, ITALIAN, WAX Whole	3-qt. pan, covered	1 inch	5–10 minutes	10–15 minutes	Tender-crisp to bite
Pieces (1 to 2 inches)	3-qt. pan, covered	1 inch	4–7 minutes	8–12 minutes	Tender-crisp to bite
BEANS, SHELLED **Cranberry, Fava**	3-qt. pan, covered	1½ inches	20–25 minutes	Do not steam	Tender to bite
Lima	3-qt. pan, covered	1½ inches	12-20 minutes	Do not steam	Tender to bite
BEETS Whole (2 to 3-inch diameter)	4 to 5-qt. kettle, covered	Water to cover	20–45 minutes	Do not steam	Tender throughout when pierced
BELGIAN ENDIVE Halved lengthwise	Wide frying pan, covered	½ inch	5–7 minutes	Do not steam	Stem end tender when pierced
BOK CHOY—See SWISS CHARD					
BROCCOLI Spears	Wide frying pan, covered	1 inch	7–12 minutes	15–20 minutes	Stalk tender when pierced
Pieces (1 inch)	Wide frying pan, covered	½ inch	3–6 minutes	8–15 minutes	Tender when pierced
BRUSSELS SPROUTS Whole (medium-size)	3-qt. pan; cover during last half of cooking time	1 inch	7–10 minutes	15–25 minutes	Stem end tender when pierced
CABBAGE, GREEN, RED, SAVOY Wedges	Wide frying pan; cover after 2 minutes	1 inch	8–12 minutes	9–14 minutes	Tender when pierced

VEGETABLE For amount for 4 servings, see chart on pages 6–13	Container	BOILING Amount of Water	Time	STEAMING Time	TEST FOR DONENESS
CARROTS Whole, baby	Wide frying pan, covered	½ inch	5–10 minutes	8–12 minutes	Tender when pierced
Whole, large	Wide frying pan, covered	1 inch	10–20 minutes	12–20 minutes	Tender when pierced
Slices (¼ inch)	Wide frying pan, covered	½ inch	5–10 minutes	5–10 minutes	Tender when pierced
CAULIFLOWER Whole (medium-size)	4 to 5-qt. kettle, covered	1 inch	15–20 minutes	20–25 minutes	Stem end tender when pierced
Flowerets	Wide frying pan, covered	½ inch	5–9 minutes	10–18 minutes	Stem end tender when pierced
Slices (¼ inch)	Wide frying pan, covered	½ cup	3–5 minutes	7–12 minutes	Tender-crisp to bite
CELERY Slices (1 inch)	Wide frying pan, covered	½ inch	5–10 minutes	8–10 minutes	Tender when pierced
CELERY HEARTS Halved lengthwise	Wide frying pan, covered	½ inch	8–12 minutes	10–14 minutes	Tender when pierced
CELERY ROOT Whole (medium-size)	3-qt. pan, covered	Water to cover	40–60 minutes	Do not steam	Tender when pierced
CHAYOTE Halved lengthwise	Wide frying pan, covered	2 inches	30–35 minutes	35–40 minutes	Tender when pierced
Slices (¼ inch)	Wide frying pan, covered	½ inch	7–9 minutes	18–22 minutes	Pale green throughout and soft to bite
CORN ON THE COB	4 to 5-qt. kettle, covered	2–3 qts.	3–5 minutes	8–10 minutes	Tender when pierced
FENNEL 3 to 4-inch diameter, halved lengthwise	Wide frying pan, covered	½–1 inch	8–10 minutes	18–22 minutes	Tender when pierced
Slices (½ inch)	Wide frying pan, covered	½ inch	5–8 minutes	10–12 minutes	Tender-crisp to bite
GREENS Collards, kale, mustard, turnip Leaves, coarsely chopped	4 to 5-qt. kettle, covered	1 inch	5–15 minutes	Do not steam	Tender to bite
KOHLRABI Whole (medium-size)	3-qt. pan, covered	1 inch	30–40 minutes	Do not steam	Tender when pierced
Slices (¼ to ½ inch)	Wide frying pan, covered	½ inch	12–25 minutes	Do not steam	Tender when pierced
LEEKS 1-inch diameter, halved lengthwise	Wide frying pan, covered	½ inch	5–8 minutes	5–8 minutes	Tender when pierced
OKRA Whole (medium-size)	3-qt. pan, covered	Water to cover	5–10 minutes	15–20 minutes	Tender when pierced
ONIONS, SMALL WHITE BOILING Whole (1 to 1½ inch diameter)	3-qt. pan, uncovered	Water to cover	15–20 minutes	20–25 minutes	Tender when pierced
PARSNIPS Whole (medium-size)	Wide frying pan, covered	1 inch	10–20 minutes	15–25 minutes	Tender when pierced
Slices (¼ inch)	Wide frying pan, covered	½ inch	5–10 minutes	7–15 minutes	Tender when pierced
PEAS, EDIBLE-POD	5-qt. kettle, uncovered	3 qts.	30 seconds	3–5 minutes	Tender-crisp to bite
PEAS, GREEN Shelled	3-qt. pan, covered	½ inch	5–10 minutes	8–12 minutes	Tender to bite
POTATOES, RED OR WHITE THIN-SKINNED Whole (3-inch diameter)	3-qt. pan, covered	1–2 inches	20–30 minutes	30–35 minutes	Tender throughout when pierced
Slices (½ inch)	3-qt. pan, covered	½–1 inch	8–10 minutes	8–10 minutes	Tender when pierced
POTATOES, SWEET OR YAMS Whole (3-inch diameter)	3-qt. pan, covered	2 inches	20–30 minutes	30–40 minutes	Tender throughout when pierced

(Continued on next page)

VEGETABLE For amount for 4 servings, see chart on pages 6–13	Container	BOILING Amount of Water	Time	STEAMING Time	TEST FOR DONENESS
RUTABAGAS Whole (3 to 4-inch diameter)	4 to 5-qt. kettle, covered	2 inches	25–35 minutes	30–45 minutes	Tender when pierced
Slices (½ inch)	Wide frying pan, covered	½–1 inch	7–10 minutes	9–12 minutes	Tender when pierced
SPINACH Leaves (whole)	4 to 5-qt. kettle, covered	Water that clings to leaves	2–4 minutes	3–5 minutes	Wilted appearance, bright color
SQUASH, SUMMER **Crookneck, pattypan, zucchini** Whole	3-qt. pan, covered	1 inch	8–12 minutes	10–12 minutes	Tender when pierced
Slices (¼ inch)	3-qt. pan, covered	½ inch	3–6 minutes	4–7 minutes	Tender when pierced
SQUASH, WINTER **Acorn, banana, butternut, Hubbard, pumpkin** Slices (½ inch)	Wide frying pan, covered	½ inch	7–9 minutes	9–12 minutes	Tender when pierced
SUNCHOKES Whole (medium-size)	3-qt. pan, covered	1 inch	10–20 minutes	15–20 minutes	Tender when pierced
Slices (¼ to ½ inch)	Wide frying pan, covered	½ inch	5–10 minutes	12–15 minutes	Tender when pierced
SWISS CHARD Stems, cut into ¼-inch slices, and leaves, shredded	Wide frying pan, covered	¼ inch	Stems 2 minutes; add leaves and cook 1–2 more minutes	Stems 3 minutes, add leaves and cook 2–4 more minutes	Tender-crisp to bite
TURNIPS Whole (2 to 3-inch diameter)	4 to 5-qt. kettle, covered	2 inches	20–30 minutes	25–35 minutes	Tender when pierced
Slices (½ inch)	Wide frying pan, covered	½ inch	6–8 minutes	7–9 minutes	Tender when pierced
YAMS—See **POTATOES, SWEET**					

Microwaving Fresh Vegetables

When it comes to cooking fresh vegetables, the microwave is truly a wonder worker. Vegetables cook in minutes, often without any nutrient-depleting liquid whatsoever. The bonuses to you are garden-fresh flavors and crispness, along with maximum retention of vitamins and minerals.

For information on selecting, storing, and preparing vegetables, see the chart beginning on page 6. Keep in mind that whole or cut-up vegetables microwave more evenly if they're of uniform size and shape. **Cook all vegetables on HIGH (100%) power.**

Covering vegetables. To hold in steam, cover the cooking dish either with the lid of the casserole or with heavy-duty plastic wrap (use only those wraps specifically described on the package as being for use in the microwave; lightweight plastic wraps may split during cooking and melt into the food). *Caution:* **When uncovering a dish after cooking, be sure to start at the edge farthest from you; escaping steam can cause burns.**

When you need only minimum moisture retention—for mushrooms and onions, for example—wax paper is a ideal cover.

Potatoes, squash, and corn on. the cob, left whole and unpeeled or unhusked, can be microwaved without any wrapping other than the natural one. Pierce potato skins before cooking to allow steam to escape (unpierced potatoes may explode).

Cooking and standing time. Cooking time depends on the freshness, moisture content, maturity, and quantity of the vegetable. (If you double the amount of vegetable, increase the initial cooking time by about 60 percent.) Remove the vegetables from the microwave after the shortest suggested cooking time and let stand for the recommended time before testing for doneness (see below). If the vegetables are still too crisp for your liking, microwave them further in 1-minute increments.

Testing for doneness. Most cooked vegetables should be tender-crisp when pierced; if overcooked, they'll dry out and become tough. Potatoes should give slightly when squeezed. Leafy vegetables should appear wilted and have bright color.

To serve. Season to taste with salt and pepper after cooking; or choose one or more of the seasonings suggested in the chart beginning on page 6.

VEGETABLE AMOUNT	CONTAINER	PREPARATION	COOKING TIME (CT) STANDING TIME (ST)
ARTICHOKE Whole 1 medium (6–8 oz.)	10-oz. custard cup	Prepare as directed on page 7. Place artichoke upside down in container. Pour in ¼ cup water and cover with plastic wrap.	CT: 5–7 minutes Before standing, lower leaves should be easy to pull away from stems with a slight tug; stem should be tender when pierced. ST: 5 minutes, covered
2 medium	9-inch round baking dish	Same as above; use ½ cup water.	CT: 8–10 minutes ST: 5 minutes, covered
3 medium	9-inch round baking dish	Same as above; use ¾ cup water.	CT: 9–11 minutes ST: 5 minutes, covered
4 medium	9-inch round baking dish	Same as above; use 1 cup water.	CT: 13–15 minutes ST: 5 minutes, covered
ASPARAGUS Spears 1 bunch (1 lb.)	7 by 11-inch baking dish	Prepare as directed on page 7. Place asparagus so buds are toward center of dish. Add 3 tablespoons water and cover with plastic wrap.	CT: 5 minutes Rearrange spears halfway through cooking, bringing center pieces to edge of dish; cover again. ST: 5 minutes, covered
Slices 1 bunch (1 lb.)	1½-qt. casserole	Prepare as directed on page 7. Cut asparagus into 1-inch slices. Add 2 tablespoons water and cover with lid or plastic wrap.	CT: 4–7 minutes Stir after 3 minutes; cover again. ST: 4–5 minutes, covered
BEANS, GREEN, ITALIAN, WAX Pieces 1 lb.	1½-qt. casserole	Prepare as directed on page 7. Cut beans into 1-inch pieces. Add ½ cup water and cover with lid or plastic wrap.	CT: 12–15 minutes Stir after every 5 minutes; cover again. ST: 5 minutes, covered Degree of tenderness depends on variety used and maturity of beans.
BEETS Whole 2 bunches (6 medium)	2-qt. casserole	Prepare as directed on page 7. Arrange beets in dish. Add 1 to 1½ cups water and cover with lid or plastic wrap.	CT: 14–16 minutes Rearrange after 7 minutes, bringing outside beets to center of casserole, cover again. ST: 5 minutes, covered Let cool until easy to handle, then peel.
BOK CHOY 1 bunch (1¼–1½ lbs.)	2-qt. casserole	Prepare as directed on page 7. Cut white stems crosswise into ¼-inch slices and place in casserole with 2 tablespoons water; cover with lid or plastic wrap. Cut leaves into 1-inch strips and add after 3 minutes cooking time.	CT: 7–8 minutes Stir in leaves after 3 minutes; cover again. ST: 2 minutes, covered
BROCCOLI Spears 1 bunch (1¼–1½ lbs.)	9 by 13-inch baking dish or 12-inch flat plate	Prepare as directed on page 7; cut into uniform spears. Peel skin off bottom 2 inches of stalks; then rinse spears and place so flowerets are toward center of dish and stalk ends are toward outside. Add 2 tablespoons water. Cover with plastic wrap.	CT: 8–10 minutes *If using baking dish*, rearrange spears halfway through cooking, bringing center pieces to edge of dish; cover again. *If using plate*, rotate plate ¼ turn. ST: 4 minutes, covered
Pieces 1 bunch (1¼–1½ lbs.)	2-qt. casserole	Prepare as directed on page 7; cut into uniform spears. Peel skin off bottom 2 inches of stalks; then rinse spears and cut into 1-inch pieces. Sprinkle with 1 tablespoon water and cover with lid or plastic wrap.	CT: 5–6 minutes Stir after 3 minutes; cover again. ST: 4 minutes, covered
BRUSSELS SPROUTS 1 lb. (about 24 medium)	1½-qt. casserole	Prepare as directed on page 7. If Brussels sprouts are not of uniform size, cut larger ones in half. Add 2 tablespoons water and cover with lid or plastic wrap.	CT: 6–7 minutes Stir after 3 minutes; cover again. ST: 3–5 minutes, covered
CABBAGE, GREEN, RED, SAVOY Shredded 1 lb. (6 cups)	2 to 3-qt. casserole	Prepare as directed on page 7. Add 2 tablespoons water and cover with lid or plastic wrap.	CT: 4–6 minutes Stir after 4 minutes; cover again. ST: 3 minutes, covered
Wedges 1 lb. (small head)	9 to 10-inch baking dish or pie plate	Prepare as directed on page 7. Arrange wedges like spokes, with large core ends toward edge of dish. Sprinkle with 2 tablespoons water and cover with lid or plastic wrap.	CT: 6–8 minutes Rotate dish ¼ turn after 3 minutes. ST: 2–3 minutes, covered
CABBAGE, NAPA 1 head (1¼–1½ lbs.)	3-qt. casserole	Cut head in half lengthwise, then cut into 1-inch pieces. Add 2 tablespoons water and cover with lid or plastic wrap.	CT: 5–6 minutes Stir after 3 minutes; cover again. ST: 3 minutes, covered

(Continued on next page)

VEGETABLE AMOUNT	CONTAINER	PREPARATION	COOKING TIME (CT) STANDING TIME (ST)
CARROTS Whole 1 lb. (1-inch diameter)	7 by 11-inch baking dish	If carrots are very tapered, cut off root ends to prevent ends from cooking faster than tops. Prepare as directed on page 7. Add ¼ cup water and cover with plastic wrap.	CT: 6–7 minutes Rotate each carrot ½ turn after 3 minutes; cover again. ST: 5 minutes, covered
Slices 1 lb. (1-inch diameter)	1-qt. casserole	Prepare as directed on page 7. Cut carrots into ¼-inch-thick slices. Add 3 tablespoons water and cover with lid or plastic wrap.	CT: 8–9 minutes Stir after 4 minutes; cover again. ST: 5 minutes, covered
CAULIFLOWER Whole 1¼ to 1½ lb. head (1 medium)	1 to 1½-qt. casserole	Prepare as directed on page 7. Place stem side down. Add 2 tablespoons water and cover with lid or plastic wrap.	CT: 10–11 minutes Turn over after 7 minutes; cover again. Before standing, stem end should be tender when pierced. ST: 5 minutes, covered
Flowerets 1¼ to 1½-lb. head (1 medium)	1½-qt. casserole	Prepare as directed on page 7. Break cauliflower into flowerets; cut larger ones in half lengthwise. Add 2 tablespoons water. Cover with lid or plastic wrap.	CT: 6–8 minutes Stir after 4 minutes; cover again. ST: 4 minutes, covered
CORN ON THE COB 1 to 6 ears	None	Be sure corn is completely enclosed in husk; secure ends with string or rubber bands. Or remove husk and silk and wrap each ear individually in plastic wrap. Arrange on paper towels on microwave floor; place 1 ear in center of oven, 2 ears side by side, 3 in a triangle, 4 ears in a square. 5 ears—place 4 in a line and 1 across top; 6 ears—place 4 in a line, 1 across top, and 1 across bottom.	CT: 3–4 minutes per ear Turn ears over halfway through cooking. ST: 2–3 minutes
GREENS **Kale** 1 bunch (about 1¼ lbs.)	3-qt. casserole	Rinse and coarsely chop greens. *Do not add water.* Cover with lid or plastic wrap.	CT: 7–8 minutes Stir after 3 minutes; cover again. ST: 2 minutes; covered
Mustard 2 bunches (about 1¼ lbs. *total*)	3-qt. casserole	Same as above	Same as above
LEEKS 1½ lbs.	8-inch square baking dish	Prepare as directed on page 11. Rinse and arrange in a single layer. *Do not add water.* Cover with plastic wrap.	CT: 5 minutes ST: 5 minutes, covered
MUSHROOMS 1 lb.	2 qt. casserole	Prepare as directed on page 11. Cut lengthwise into ¼-inch slices. Add 2 tablespoons water, or 2 tablespoons butter or margarine cut into 6 pieces. Cover with lid or wax paper.	CT: 4–6 minutes Stir after 2 minutes; cover again. ST: 2 minutes, covered
ONIONS Quarters 1 lb. (2 large)	1-qt. casserole	Prepare as directed on page 11. Cut into quarters (eighths, if extra large). *Do not add water.* Cover with lid or wax paper.	CT: 5–6 minutes Stir after 2 minutes; cover again. ST: 5 minutes, covered
Slices 1 lb.	1-qt. casserole	Prepare as directed on page 11. Slice ¼ inch thick and separate into rings. Add 2 tablespoons water, or 2 tablespoons butter or margarine cut into 6 pieces. Cover with lid or wax paper.	CT: 5–6 minutes Stir after 2 minutes; cover again. (To make onions sweet, cook for 10 minutes, stirring after every 3 minutes; cover again.) ST: 5 minutes, covered
Whole (small boiling onions) 8 to 12	1-qt. casserole	Peel as directed on page 11. *Do not add water.* Cover with lid or plastic wrap.	CT: 4–6 minutes Stir after 2 minutes; cover again. ST: 5 minutes, covered
PARSNIPS 1 lb. (4 medium)	1½-qt. casserole	Prepare as directed on page 11. Cut into ½-inch cubes. Add ¼ cup water and cover with lid or plastic wrap.	CT: 8–9 minutes Stir after 4 minutes; cover again. ST: 5 minutes, covered
PEAS, EDIBLE-POD 1 lb.	2-qt. casserole	Prepare as directed on page 11. Rinse. *Do not add water.* Cover with lid or plastic wrap.	CT: 4–5 minutes Stir after 2 minutes; cover again. ST: 4 minutes, covered
PEAS, GREEN Unshelled About 2½ lbs. (to yield 2½ cups shelled)	1½-qt. casserole	Prepare as directed on page 11. Add ¼ cup water and cover with lid or plastic wrap.	CT: 8–12 minutes Stir after 5 minutes; cover again. ST: 5 minutes, covered

VEGETABLE AMOUNT	CONTAINER	PREPARATION	COOKING TIME (CT) STANDING TIME (ST)
POTATOES, RUSSET 1 to 6 potatoes (8 oz. *each*)	None	Pierce skin on 4 sides with a fork or knife. Place on paper towels on microwave floor. Arrange at least 1 inch apart as follows: 1 potato in center of oven 2 potatoes side by side 3 potatoes in a triangle 4 potatoes like spokes 5 potatoes as above 6 potatoes as above	CT: 4–5 minutes 6–8 minutes 8–10 minutes 10–12 minutes 12–15 minutes 15–20 minutes Turn potatoes over halfway through cooking. After cooking, potatoes should give slightly when squeezed. ST: 5–10 minutes, wrapped in a clean towel or in foil.
POTATOES, SWEET (OR YAMS) 1 to 6 fairly round potatoes (about 8 oz. *each*)	None	Prepare and arrange as for russet potatoes (see above). 1 sweet potato 2 or 3 sweet potatoes 4 or 5 sweet potatoes 6 sweet potatoes	CT: 4–5 minutes 6–7 minutes 8–12 minutes 12–16 minutes Follow directions for russet potatoes (see above). ST: 5–10 minutes, wrapped in a clean towel or in foil.
SPINACH 1 lb.	3-qt. casserole	Prepare as directed on page 13. *Do not add water.* Cover with lid or plastic wrap.	CT: 5–7 minutes Stir after 3 minutes; cover again. ST: 2 minutes, covered
SPROUTS, BEAN 1 lb.	2-qt. casserole	Rinse in cold water just before using; drain. *Do not add water.* Cover with lid or plastic wrap.	CT: 4–5 minutes Stir after 2 minutes; cover again. ST: 2 minutes, covered
SQUASH, SPAGHETTI 1 medium (1¼ lbs.)	9 by 13-inch baking dish	Prepare as directed on page 13. Cut in half lengthwise and remove seeds. Place squash, hollow side up, in dish. Spread cut surfaces with 1 to 2 tablespoons butter or margarine. Cover with plastic wrap.	CT: 10–12 minutes Rotate each piece ½ turn after 5 minutes; cover again. ST: 5 minutes, covered
SQUASH, SUMMER Crookneck, pattypan, zucchini 1 lb.	1½-qt. casserole	Prepare as directed on page 13. Slice squash ¼ inch thick. Add 2 tablespoons butter or margarine cut into 6 pieces. Cover with lid or plastic wrap.	CT: 6–7 minutes Stir after 3 minutes; cover again. ST: 3 minutes, covered
SQUASH, WINTER Acorn or butternut 2 medium (1½ lbs. *each*)	10 to 12-inch flat plate	Prepare as directed on page 13. Cut in half lengthwise and remove seeds. Place squash, hollow side up, on plate with fleshy portion toward edge of dish. Spread cut surfaces with 1 to 2 tablespoons butter or margarine. Cover with plastic wrap.	CT: 10–12 minutes Rotate plate ¼ turn after 5 minutes. ST: 5 minutes, covered
Banana 1 lb. slice	7 by 11-inch baking dish	Prepare as directed on page 13. Spread cut surface with 1 to 2 tablespoons butter or margarine. Cover with plastic wrap.	CT: 12–13 minutes Rotate dish ½ turn after 6 minutes. ST: 5 minutes, covered
SWISS CHARD 1 bunch (1¼–1½ lbs.)	2-qt. casserole	Prepare as directed on page 13. Cut white stems crosswise into ¼-inch slices and place in casserole with 2 tablespoons water; cover with lid or plastic wrap. Cut leaves into 1-inch strips and add after 3 minutes cooking time.	CT: 7–8 minutes Stir in leaves after 3 minutes; cover again. ST: 2 minutes, covered
TURNIPS 1 lb. (2 or 3 medium)	1½-qt. casserole	Prepare as directed on page 13. Cut into ½-inch cubes. Add 3 tablespoons water and cover with lid or plastic wrap.	CT: 7–9 minutes Stir after 3 minutes; cover again. ST: 3 minutes, covered
YAMS See **POTATOES, SWEET**			

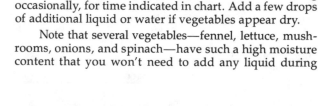

Stir-frying & Butter-steaming Fresh Vegetables

Stir-frying and butter-steaming are similar techniques that quickly produce cooked vegetables with tender-crisp texture, bright color, and rich, natural flavor. Whether you stir-fry or butter-steam in a wok or frying pan, the basic procedure is the same.

To stir-fry or butter-steam. Prepare vegetables (see chart beginning on page 6); then cut as indicated in chart below. Place a wok or wide frying pan over high heat; when wok is hot, add salad oil or butter (depending on method of cooking) and cut-up vegetables. Cook, uncovered, stirring constantly, for time given in chart. Add specified amount of liquid; then cover and cook, stirring occasionally, for time indicated in chart. Add a few drops of additional liquid or water if vegetables appear dry.

Note that several vegetables—fennel, lettuce, mushrooms, onions, and spinach—have such a high moisture content that you won't need to add any liquid during cooking. Don't cover the pan when cooking fennel and mushrooms; they'll be ready to serve after just a few minutes of uncovered cooking.

We do not suggest stir-frying those vegetables that taste better when cooked in butter.

Two secrets to success. *Never crowd the wok or frying pan.* Cook no more than 5 cups cut-up vegetable in a 12 to 14-inch wok or 10-inch frying pan. To prepare more servings than you can cook at one time, have ready the total amount of cut-up vegetables you'll need, and cook in two batches. The cooking process is so fast that you can keep the first portion warm, without flavor loss, while the second portion cooks.

Use highest heat so the vegetables begin cooking at once: a slow start means slow cooking. As the vegetables cook, all or most of the liquid evaporates; because there's no cooking liquid to drain off, vitamins and minerals are retained.

Testing for doneness. Cooking time will vary, depending on the freshness and maturity of the vegetables and on individual preference. Taste after the minimum cooking time; if you prefer a softer texture, continue cooking, tasting frequently, until vegetables are done to your liking.

To serve. Season to taste with salt and pepper; or choose one of the seasonings suggested in the chart beginning on page 6.

VEGETABLE 4 to 5 cups cut-up vegetable	TABLESPOONS salad oil to stir-fry OR	TABLESPOONS butter or margarine to butter-steam	MINUTES to cook and stir, uncovered	TABLESPOONS regular-strength chicken or beef broth or water	MINUTES to cook covered
ASPARAGUS Cut into ½-inch diagonal slices	1	2	1	1–2	2–3
BEANS, GREEN, ITALIAN, WAX Cut into 1-inch pieces	1	2	1	4	4–7
BEET GREENS Shredded	Do not stir-fry	2	1	1–2	2–3
BEETS Cut into ¼-inch slices	Do not stir-fry	2	1	6	5–6
BOK CHOY See **SWISS CHARD**					
BROCCOLI Cut into ¼-inch slices	1	2	1	3–5	3–5
BRUSSELS SPROUTS Cut in half lengthwise	Do not stir-fry	2	1	3–5	3–5
CABBAGE, GREEN, RED, SAVOY Shredded	1	2	1	2	3–4
CABBAGE, NAPA Cut white part into 1-inch slices; shred leaves and add during last 2–3 minutes of cooking time	1	2	1–2	2	4–5
CARROTS Cut into ¼-inch slices	1	2	1	2–3	3–5
CAULIFLOWER Flowerets, cut into ¼-inch slices	1	3	1	3–4	4–5

VEGETABLE 4 to 5 cups cut-up vegetable	TABLESPOONS salad oil to stir-fry OR	TABLESPOONS butter or margarine to butter-steam	MINUTES to cook and stir, uncovered	TABLESPOONS regular-strength chicken or beef broth or water	MINUTES to cook covered
CELERY Cut into ¼-inch slices	1	2	1	1–2	1–3
CELERY ROOT Cut into ¼-inch slices	Do not stir-fry	2	1	3–4	2–4
CHAYOTE Cut into ¼-inch slices	Do not stir-fry	3	1	4–6	6–8
CUCUMBERS, ARMENIAN, ENGLISH, MARKETER Cut into ¼-inch slices	Do not stir-fry	2	1	1	2–2½
FENNEL Cut into ¼-inch slices	1	2	2–3	No liquid necessary	No covered cooking necessary
KOHLRABI Cut into ⅛-inch slices	Do not stir-fry	3	1	7	6–8
LEEKS White part only, cut into ¼-inch slices	1	2	1	3–4	3
LETTUCE, ICEBERG Shredded	Do not stir-fry	2	½	No liquid necessary	2–3
MUSHROOMS Cut into ¼-inch slices	1	2	3–4	No liquid necessary	No covered cooking necessary
ONIONS, DRY Cut into ¼-inch slices	1	2	1	No liquid necessary	3–4
PARSNIPS Cut into ¼-inch slices	2	4	1	6–8	4–6
PEAS, EDIBLE-POD	1	2	3	1	½
PEAS, GREEN Shelled	1	2	1	3–4	2–3
PEPPERS, GREEN OR RED BELL Cut into 1-inch pieces	1	2	1	2–3	3–5
RUTABAGAS Cut into ¼-inch slices	1	2	1	4–5	5–6
SPINACH Leaves, whole or coarsely chopped	1	2	½	No liquid necessary	2–3
SPROUTS, BEAN	1	2	1	1	½–1½
SQUASH, SUMMER **Crookneck, pattypan, zucchini** Cut into ¼-inch slices	1	2	1	2–4	3–4
SQUASH, WINTER **Banana, Hubbard, pumpkin** Cut into 1-inch cubes	Do not stir-fry	2	1	3–5	6–8
SUNCHOKES Cut into ¼-inch slices	Do not stir-fry	2	1	2–3	3–5
SWISS CHARD Cut stems into ¼-inch slices; shred leaves and add during last 2–3 minutes of cooking time	1	2	1	1	3½–4½
TURNIP GREENS Shredded	Do not stir-fry	2	1	1–2	3–5
TURNIPS Cut into ¼-inch slices	1	2	1	4–5	4–5

Baking & Roasting Fresh Vegetables

Certain vegetables cook to perfection in the oven. Baking or roasting accentuates the naturally mellow-sweet flavor and preserves the nutritional value of vegetables such as corn, potatoes, and squash. At the same time, the dry oven heat tames the pungency of other vegetables such as garlic and onions.

Oven-cooking vegetables. When you tuck vegetables into the same oven with beef or chicken, you save energy—your own included. The vegetables require minimal preparation and cook with little or no atten-tion. Some vegetables—onions and potatoes, for example—can be roasted alongside the meat in the pan drippings. In this case, use the oven temperature specified for roasting the meat and add 20 to 30 minutes to the cooking time listed in the chart for the vegetables.

Never overcrowd the oven; the heat needs ample room to circulate. As long as you observe this rule, you can bake ten potatoes as quickly as one.

To adapt the following chart for convection oven baking, lower the oven temperature by 25° or 50°; test for doneness at the minimum suggested time.

To serve. Season baked or roasted vegetables to taste with salt and pepper; or choose one or more of the seasonings suggested in the chart beginning on page 6. *Exception:* Don't serve roasted garlic as you would other vegetables. Pluck garlic cloves from the head and squeeze each to release the cooked garlic. Serve on dinner rolls, cooked meat, or other vegetables.

VEGETABLE PREPARATION	OVEN TEMPERATURE	TIME	TEST FOR DONENESS
BEETS—2 to 3-inch diameter Scrub beets; pat dry. Do not peel. Wrap each beet in heavy-duty foil.	375°	1–1¼ hours	Tender when pierced
CARROTS—Medium-size Scrub well or peel; cut into 1-inch diagonal slices. Arrange in a shallow layer in a baking dish; generously dot with butter or margarine.	325°, covered Stir several times.	40–50 minutes	Tender when pierced
CORN ON THE COB—Large ears Remove husk and silk. Rub kernels with butter or margarine. Wrap each ear in heavy-duty foil.	375°	30—35 minutes	Tender when pierced
EGGPLANT—Large Scrub; pat dry. Cut into ½-inch-thick slices; brush all sides with salad oil. Arrange in a single layer in a shallow baking pan.	425°–450°, uncovered	20–30 minutes	Well browned and tender when pierced
GARLIC—Large heads Place whole, unpeeled heads in a greased dish.	325°, uncovered	1 hour	Tender when pierced
ONIONS, DRY—Medium-size Peel; stand upright in a close-fitting baking dish. Drizzle with melted butter or margarine.	350°, uncovered Baste several times with butter.	30–45 minutes	Tender when pierced
PARSNIPS—Medium-size Peel; cut into sticks ½ inch by 3 to 4 inches. Arrange in a shallow layer in a baking dish; generously dot with butter or margarine.	325°, covered Stir several times.	45–60 minutes	Tender when pierced
PEPPERS, GREEN OR RED BELL—Large Cut lengthwise into quarters; discard stem and seeds. Rinse. Arrange, skin side down, in a greased, close-fitting dish; drizzle with salad or olive oil.	375°, uncovered	40–45 minutes	Tender when pierced
POTATOES, RUSSET OR THIN-SKINNED—Medium-size Scrub; pat dry. Pierce skin in several places; rub with butter or margarine. Place on oven rack (potatoes shouldn't touch each other).	400°, uncovered	50–60 minutes	Soft when squeezed
POTATOES, SWEET (OR YAMS)—Medium-size Scrub; pat dry. Pierce skin in several places; rub with butter or margarine. Arrange in a single layer on a rimmed baking sheet.	400°, uncovered	45–50 minutes	Soft when squeezed
RUTABAGAS—Medium-size Peel; cut into ¼-inch slices. Arrange in a shallow layer in a baking dish. Generously dot with butter or margarine; sprinkle lightly with water.	400°, covered	30–45 minutes	Tender when pierced
SQUASH, SPAGHETTI—Medium-size Rinse; pierce in several places. Place on a rimmed baking sheet.	350°, uncovered Turn over after 45 minutes.	1½ hours	Shell gives to pressure

VEGETABLE PREPARATION	OVEN TEMPERATURE	TIME	TEST FOR DONENESS
SQUASH, WINTER			
Acorn, butternut—Medium-size Cut in half lengthwise. Scrape out seeds and stringy portions. Place, cut side down, in a greased baking dish.	400°–450°, uncovered	30–40 minutes	Flesh tender when pierced
Banana, Hubbard—Large pieces Cut into serving-size pieces. Scrape out seeds and stringy portions. Place, cut side down, in a greased baking dish.	400°–450°, uncovered	30–40 minutes	Flesh tender when pierced
Pumpkin—9–11 pounds Cut in half lengthwise. Scrape out seeds and stringy portions. Place, cut side down, on a greased rimmed baking sheet.	350°, uncovered	1–1¼ hours	Flesh tender when pierced
TOMATOES—Medium-size Core and cut in half crosswise; squeeze out juice and seeds. Place, cut side up, in a baking dish. Drizzle with olive oil or salad oil.	400°, uncovered	20–25 minutes	Soft throughout
TURNIPS—See **RUTABAGAS**			
YAMS—See **POTATOES, SWEET**			

Grilling Fresh Vegetables

It's a simple matter to grill vegetables on the barbecue alongside the main course. You can prepare the vegetables ahead of time and have the foil-wrapped packets waiting to put on the grill when the fire is ready.

To grill. Rinse vegetables thoroughly but do not pat dry—water that clings creates enough moisture to steam most vegetables. Place up to 4 servings of the vegetable (see chart beginning on page 6) on a sheet of heavy-duty foil (if grilling more than 4 servings, prepare several sheets; wrap potatoes and corn on the cob individually). Evenly dot with butter or margarine, using 2 tablespoons for every 4 servings.

Wrap vegetables tightly in foil and place on a grill 4 to 6 inches above a solid bed of medium-glowing coals. Cook, shifting packets occasionally so vegetables cook evenly; test for doneness at minimum suggested time.

To serve. Season to taste with salt and pepper; or choose one or more of the seasonings suggested in the chart beginning on page 6.

VEGETABLE	TIME	TEST FOR DONENESS
ASPARAGUS Spears	15–20 minutes	Tender when pierced
BEANS, GREEN, ITALIAN, WAX Whole	20 minutes	Tender-crisp to bite
CARROTS Cut into 1-inch slices	25–30 minutes	Tender when pierced
CORN ON THE COB Remove husk and silk, wrap individually	15–20 minutes	Tender when pierced
PEAS, GREEN Shelled	20 minutes	Tender to bite
POTATOES, RED OR WHITE THIN-SKINNED Small whole; pierce skin	50–55 minutes	Tender throughout when pierced
POTATOES, RUSSET Medium-size whole; pierce skin, wrap individually	1 hour	Soft when squeezed
SQUASH, SUMMER Crookneck, pattypan, zucchini Cut into 1-inch slices	20–25 minutes	Tender when pierced
SQUASH, WINTER Banana, Hubbard Peel; cut into 1 by 6-inch spears	25–30 minutes	Tender when pierced

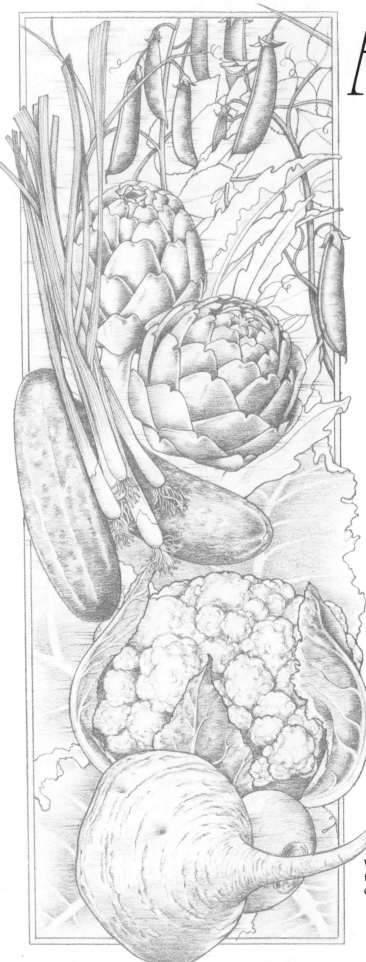

Appetizers

&

First Courses

L *aunch an elegant dinner or an informal gathering with light, fresh vegetable starters. From simple pick-up-and-munch fare to an assortment of hot treats, these appetizers and first-course offerings will suit any occasion.*

Pair raw or briefly cooked vegetables with a variety of tasty dipping sauces, or salute the season by using the pick of the produce market in finger-food combinations. You'll find appetizers that serve a crowd, as well as easy but impressive first courses to begin a leisurely sit-down dinner.

WHET APPETITES with garden-fresh vegetables, many of them delicious raw: edible-pod peas, artichokes, green onions, marketer cucumbers, cauliflower, turnips, jicama.

Jicama Crisps

Imported from Mexico, jicama (*hee*-cah-muh) is a brown root with crisp white flesh that tastes like a juicy water chestnut. Street vendors in Mexico sell jicama crisps like these as a refreshing snack.

    1 tablespoon salt
    ¼ teaspoon chili powder
    1 lime
    1 to 1½ pounds jicama

In a small bowl, blend salt with chili powder. Cut lime into wedges. Peel jicama and slice ¼ to ½ inch thick; arrange with lime wedges on a serving tray. To eat, rub lime over each jicama slice and dip into seasoned salt. Makes 6 to 8 servings.

Italian Eggplant Relish

Pine nuts and pimentos add interest to this tangy mixture of eggplant, onion, and celery. Spoon it into small crisp lettuce cups to eat out of hand.

    ½ cup olive oil or salad oil
    1 eggplant (about 1¼ lbs.), cut into
      ¾-inch cubes
    1½ cups sliced celery
    1 large onion, chopped
    3 cloves garlic, minced or pressed
    ¼ cup tomato paste
    1 cup water
    2 teaspoons sugar
    ¼ cup red wine vinegar
    1 cup sliced ripe olives
    2 tablespoons capers, drained well
    ½ cup *each* chopped pimentos and pine
      nuts
      Small crisp lettuce cups or Melba toast

Heat oil in a wide frying pan over medium heat; add eggplant, cover, and cook until eggplant begins to sweat (about 5 minutes). Uncover and continue to cook, stirring often, until eggplant is browned (about 5 more minutes). Stir in celery, onion, and garlic and cook, stirring often, until onion is soft.

In a small bowl, stir together tomato paste, water, sugar, and vinegar; stir into eggplant mixture. Cook, stirring often, until mixture thickens and eggplant is very soft (about 10 minutes). Remove from heat and stir in olives, capers, and pimentos. Let cool; then cover and refrigerate for at least 1 day or up to 1 week.

Spoon mixture into a serving dish and sprinkle with pine nuts. Serve cold or at room temperature; spoon into lettuce cups or spread on Melba toast. Makes about 4 cups.

Cheese-Mushroom Fingers

Mushrooms, onion, and green pepper bake together in this herb-seasoned cheese custard—delicious warm or at room temperature.

Cut into bite-size morsels, the custard provides hors d'oeuvres for a crowd. You can make this appetizer ahead and reheat it just before serving, if you like.

    ½ cup (¼ lb.) butter or margarine
    1 pound mushrooms, sliced
    1 large onion, chopped
    2 cloves garlic, minced or pressed
    1 large green pepper, seeded and chopped
    10 eggs
    1 pint (2 cups) small curd cottage cheese
    4 cups (1 lb.) shredded jack cheese
    ½ cup all-purpose flour
    1 teaspoon baking powder
    ¾ teaspoon *each* ground nutmeg, dry basil,
      and salt

Melt butter in a wide frying pan over medium-high heat. Add mushrooms, onion, and garlic; cook, stirring, until onion and mushrooms are soft. Add green pepper and cook, stirring, for 1 more minute; set aside.

In a large bowl, beat together eggs, cottage cheese, jack cheese, flour, baking powder, nutmeg, basil, and salt until blended. Stir in mushroom mixture and turn into a well-greased 10 by 15-inch rimmed baking sheet. Bake in a 350° oven for 35 minutes or until set when lightly touched in center.

Let cool on a rack for at least 15 minutes; then cut into ¾ by 2-inch fingers. Serve warm or at room temperature. If made ahead, cover and refrigerate for up to 2 days.

To serve warm, reheat, uncovered, in a 350° oven for 15 minutes or until heated through. Makes about 8 dozen appetizers.

Vegetable-Cheese Nachos

In this twist on a favorite Mexican-style snack, crisp vegetables substitute for tortilla chips as scoops for melted cheese.

> **4 cups assorted cut-up vegetables (suggestions follow)**
> **2 cups (8 oz.) shredded jack or Cheddar cheese**
> **2 to 3 tablespoons *each* canned diced green chiles and sliced ripe olives**

Arrange vegetable pieces on a heatproof platter. Sprinkle evenly with cheese, chiles, and olives. Broil 4 to 6 inches below heat until cheese is melted (5 to 7 minutes). Makes 6 servings.

Assorted vegetables. Choose 2 or more from the following: **carrot** or **celery** sticks; **zucchini** or **crookneck squash** rounds; **green** or **red bell pepper** strips; **jicama** or **turnip** sticks. Cut vegetables thick enough to scoop up cheese.

Crisp Potato Skins

Serve crunchy fried potato skins unadorned, or dress them up with a topping of cheese and salsa or peanut butter and chutney as described at right. Reserve the insides for Mashed Potatoes (page 87) or Potatoes in a Pastry Shell (page 82).

> **5 large russet potatoes (about 3 lbs. *total*)**
> **Salad oil or butter (see below)**
> **Salt**

Scrub potatoes and pierce each with a fork. Bake in a 400° oven for 1 hour or until potatoes feel soft when squeezed.

When cool enough to touch, cut in half lengthwise, then cut each half crosswise into quarters. With a spoon, scoop flesh from skins, leaving a ⅛-inch-thick shell; reserve flesh for other uses. Deep-fry or oven-fry skins.

To deep-fry: Pour salad oil into a deep 3 to 4-quart pan to a depth of 2 inches; heat to 400° on a deep-frying thermometer. Add potato skins, about 6 at a time, and cook until crisp and golden (about 1 minute). Remove with a slotted spoon and drain on paper towels. Repeat with remaining skins.

To oven-fry: Brush potato skins inside and out with about ⅓ cup butter or margarine, melted. Place skins, cut side up, in a single layer on a 10 by 15-inch baking sheet. Bake in a 500° oven for about 12 minutes or until crisp.

Sprinkle deep-fried or oven-fried skins with salt, if desired, and serve hot. If made ahead, let stand at room temperature, uncovered, for up to 6 hours. To reheat, place skins, cut side up, in a single layer on a 10 by 15-inch baking sheet. Bake in a 400° oven for about 8 minutes or until crisp. Makes 4 to 6 servings.

Salsa Potato Skins. In a small bowl, stir together 1 can (8 oz.) **tomato sauce,** 1 can (4 oz.) **diced green chiles,** and ¼ cup chopped **green onions** (including tops). Pour salsa into a small serving bowl. If made ahead, cover and refrigerate until next day.

Bake potatoes as directed for **Crisp Potato Skins,** but cut potatoes lengthwise into quarters instead of in half; do not cut crosswise. Deep-fry or oven-fry as directed.

Place hot skins, cut side up, in a single layer on a 10 by 15-inch baking sheet. Evenly distribute ¾ cup *each* shredded **jack cheese** and **Cheddar cheese** over skins. Broil 4 inches below heat until cheeses are melted (about 2 minutes). Arrange skins on a tray and accompany with salsa for dipping. Serve hot. Makes 4 to 6 servings.

Peanut Butter & Chutney Potato Skins. Prepare **Crisp Potato Skins,** deep-fried or oven-fried as directed. Arrange hot skins, cut side up, in a single layer on a 10 by 15-inch baking sheet. Spoon 1 teaspoon **crunchy peanut butter** onto each skin; top with ½ teaspoon **Major Grey's chutney.** Broil 4 inches below heat until peanut butter begins to melt (about 2 minutes). Serve hot. Makes 4 to 6 servings.

Roasted Garlic Heads

Slowly roasted garlic has a surprisingly mild flavor—in fact, it's almost sweet . . . not to mention the fact that it's almost breathless. To serve it as an appetizer, squeeze the buttery contents of the cloves onto crackers or thin zucchini slices. Or you can spread the roasted garlic over cooked vegetables such as green beans, broccoli, asparagus, or baked potatoes.

> **2 heads garlic, unpeeled**
> **Crackers or thin zucchini slices**

Place garlic heads on a lightly greased pan. Bake in a 325° oven for 1 hour or until soft throughout (to test, pierce all the way to head centers with a wooden skewer). Let cool slightly; then pluck off individual cloves and squeeze onto crackers. Makes 6 servings.

Garlicky Pea Pods

For zesty simplicity, dip fresh, sweet edible-pod peas into hot, garlicky butter.

- 1 **pound edible-pod peas**
- ½ **cup (¼ lb.) butter or margarine**
- 2 **to 4 cloves garlic, minced or pressed**
- 1 **tablespoon minced parsley**
  Salt and pepper

Break off ends of peas; remove and discard strings. Rinse peas well, pat dry, and place in a plastic bag. Refrigerate for at least 4 hours or until next day.

Melt butter in a small pan over medium-low heat. Stir in garlic and parsley; season to taste with salt and pepper. Pour hot butter mixture into a small warm serving bowl. Arrange peas on a serving tray and offer butter mixture for dipping. Makes 4 to 6 servings.

Herbed Mushrooms

Serve hot, buttery mushrooms, fragrant with aromatic herbs and dry sherry, when you want a no-fuss appetizer to complement cheeses.

- 1½ **pounds mushrooms,** *each* **about 1 inch in diameter**
- 2 **tablespoons butter or margarine**
- 1 **small onion, finely chopped**
- 1 **teaspoon** *each* **dry basil and oregano leaves**
- ¼ **teaspoon** *each* **thyme leaves, garlic salt, and liquid hot pepper seasoning**
- 2 **tablespoons lime juice**
- ¼ **cup dry sherry**

Remove mushroom stems and reserve for other uses. Melt butter in a wide frying pan over medium heat; add whole mushroom caps and onion; cook until soft. Add basil, oregano, thyme, garlic

salt, hot pepper seasoning, lime juice, and sherry. (At this point, you may transfer mushroom mixture to a bowl and let cool; then cover and refrigerate for up to 2 days.)

Just before serving, cook mushroom mixture, uncovered, over medium-high heat, stirring often, until liquid is reduced to 3 tablespoons. Keep warm over canned heat or an alcohol burner. Provide wooden picks for spearing mushrooms. Makes about 6 dozen appetizers.

Zucchini-Cheese Appetizer Squares

Ideal for a large gathering, this zucchini-flecked cheese custard makes dozens of tasty appetizers. Serve them warm, at room temperature, or cold.

- ¼ **cup sesame seeds**
- ¼ **cup salad oil**
- 1 **small onion, chopped**
- 1 **clove garlic, minced or pressed**
- 2½ **cups shredded zucchini**
- 6 **eggs, lightly breaten**
- ⅓ **cup fine dry bread crumbs**
- ½ **teaspoon** *each* **salt, dry basil, and oregano leaves**
- ¼ **teaspoon pepper**
- 3 **cups (12 oz.) shredded Cheddar cheese**
- ½ **cup grated Parmesan cheese**

In a wide frying pan over medium heat, toast sesame seeds, shaking pan frequently, until golden (about 2 minutes); remove from pan and set aside.

Heat oil in pan over medium-high heat. Add onion and garlic; cook, stirring, until soft (about 4 minutes). Add zucchini and cook until tender-crisp (about 3 more minutes).

In a large bowl, mix eggs, bread crumbs, salt, basil, oregano, pepper, Cheddar cheese, and zucchini mixture. Spread in a greased 9 by 13-inch baking pan. Sprinkle with Parmesan cheese and sesame seeds. Bake in a 325° oven for 30 minutes or until set when lightly touched in center. Let cool on a rack for at least 15 minutes.

Cut into 1-inch squares and serve warm or at room temperature; or cover and refrigerate, and serve cold. Makes about 10 dozen appetizers.

Zucchini or Potato Hot Tots

Enjoy cooked rounds of zucchini or potato, topped with an herb and cheese-laced mayonnaise, as a tasty appetizer or a quick side dish.

> 3 **medium-size zucchini or thin-skinned potatoes, sliced ¾ inch thick**
> ⅓ **cup mayonnaise**
> ¼ **cup minced green onions (including tops)**
> ½ **cup grated Parmesan cheese**
> **Dash of pepper**
> ½ **teaspoon oregano leaves**
> ⅛ **teaspoon garlic powder**
> **About 3 tablespoons fine dry bread crumbs**
> **Paprika**

Arrange zucchini or potato slices on a steaming rack. Steam as directed on pages 17 and 18, but cook just until barely tender (about 5 minutes for zucchini, 12 to 15 minutes for potatoes). Let cool; then blot dry with paper towels and set aside.

In a small bowl, mix mayonnaise, onions, cheese, pepper, oregano, and garlic powder until well blended. Spread mayonnaise mixture evenly over one side of each vegetable slice. Dip tops in bread crumbs, then sprinkle with paprika. Arrange slices in a single layer on a baking sheet. (At this point, you may cover and refrigerate until next day; bring to room temperature before proceeding.)

Broil vegetables 4 inches below heat until lightly browned (3 to 6 minutes). Makes about 24 zucchini slices or about 12 potato slices.

Crisp-fried Onions

These sweet, golden onions are especially light and fragile. The secret? Before frying, they receive only a dusting of flour instead of the typical batter coating. Serve them warm as a chewy-crisp snack with a glass of wine, or use as a topping for broiled meats, open-faced sandwiches, or hot vegetables. You can fry the onions ahead, then reheat to serve.

> 2 **large onions (about 1 lb. *total*)**
> ½ **cup all-purpose flour**
> **Salad oil**
> **Salt**

Thinly slice onions, then separate into rings. Place flour in a bag, add onions, and shake to coat.

Pour oil into a deep 2½ to 3-quart pan to a depth of 1½ inches. Heat to 300° on a deep-frying thermometer. Add onions, about a fourth at a time, and cook, stirring often, until golden (about 5 minutes.) Oil temperature will drop at first but rise again as onions brown; regulate heat to maintain temperature at 300°.

Remove onions with a slotted spoon and drain on paper towels; discard any scorched bits. Pile in a napkin-lined basket or on a plate; sprinkle with salt and serve warm.

If made ahead, let cool completely, package airtight, and refrigerate for up to 3 days. To reheat, spread in a single layer in a shallow pan; heat in a 350° oven for 2 to 3 minutes. Makes about 6 cups.

Cheddar-Asparagus Roll-ups

Welcome spring with these buttery treats. Inside each toasted roll, melted Cheddar cheese coats an asparagus spear.

> 20 **asparagus spears**
> 6 to 8 **ounces sharp Cheddar cheese**
> 1 **loaf (1 lb.) sliced sandwich bread**
> ¾ **cup (¼ lb. plus 4 tablespoons) butter or margarine, softened**
> 1 **tablespoon chopped parsley**
> ½ **teaspoon dill weed**
> 3 **tablespoons sliced green onions (including tops)**
> **Salt and pepper**

Snap off and discard tough ends of asparagus; peel stalks, if desired. Boil asparagus according to directions on page 16. Drain well and set aside.

Cut cheese into sticks 2½ to 3 inches long and ¼ to ½ inch wide. Trim crusts from 20 bread slices and flatten each slice slightly with a rolling pin. In a small bowl, mix ½ cup of the butter with parsley, dill, and onions; season to taste with salt and pepper. Spread butter mixture evenly over one side of each bread slice; then top each with an asparagus spear and a cheese stick. Roll up each slice, secure with a wooden pick, and arrange on an ungreased baking sheet.

Melt remaining 4 tablespoons butter and brush evenly over rolls. Broil about 5 inches below heat until golden (3 to 5 minutes). Makes 20 appetizers.

Distinctive Dips
for Crunchy Vegetables

Crisp, fresh raw vegetables contrast deliciously with creamy smooth dips.

Ahead of time, make your favorite dip; then prepare 1 to 2 cups of vegetables for each serving, choosing three or more of the following: asparagus spears, green beans, broccoli flowerets, carrot sticks, cauliflowerets, celery sticks, cucumber spears, fennel slices, edible-pod peas, green or red bell pepper strips, radishes, zucchini or crookneck squash spears, cherry tomatoes, turnip slices.

Creamy Dill Dip

- ⅔ cup *each* **mayonnaise and sour cream**
- 2 tablespoons **chopped parsley**
- 2½ teaspoons *each* **dill weed and minced onion**
- 1 teaspoon **seasoned salt**

In a small bowl, combine mayonnaise and sour cream. Add parsley, dill, onion, and salt; mix well. Cover and refrigerate for at least 4 hours or until next day. Serve cold. Makes about 1⅓ cups.

Zippy Hot Cheese Dip

- 1 medium-size **tomato, peeled, seeded, and chopped**
- ¼ cup **chopped green onions (including tops)**
- 3 to 4 tablespoons **diced green chiles**
- ½ teaspoon *each* **salt and ground coriander**
- 1 box (2 lbs.) **pasteurized process cheese spread**

In a small bowl, combine tomato, onions, chiles, salt, and coriander; set aside.

Place cheese in a 3-quart pan; stir over medium-low heat until cheese is melted and smooth. Stir in tomato mixture. Serve in a chafing dish over hot water or in a ceramic fondue pot over a low alcohol flame. Makes 5 cups.

Blue Cheese & Sour Cream Dip

- ½ pint (1 cup) **sour cream**
- ⅓ cup **mayonnaise**
- 3 tablespoons **lemon juice**
- 4 ounces **blue-veined cheese**
- 1 clove **garlic, minced or pressed**
- ½ teaspoon **salt**

In a blender or food processor, combine sour cream, mayonnaise, lemon juice, cheese, garlic, and salt. Whirl until smooth. Cover and refrigerate for at least 2 hours or until next day. Makes 2 cups.

Cucumber–Cottage Cheese Dip

- 1 large **cucumber**
- 2 envelopes **instant onion soup (*each* amount for 1 serving)**
- 3 hard-cooked **egg yolks**
- ½ cup **cottage cheese with chives**
- ¼ cup **mayonnaise**
- 1 tablespoon **prepared horseradish**
- ½ medium-size **avocado**
- 1 teaspoon **lemon juice**
  Liquid hot pepper seasoning
  Salt

Peel cucumber and cut into small cubes; you should have about 1½ cups. In a blender or food processor, combine cucumber, soup mix, egg yolks, cottage cheese, mayonnaise, and horseradish. Whirl until smooth.

Peel and dice avocado and add to cucumber mixture along with lemon juice; then sprinkle with hot pepper seasoning and salt to taste. Whirl until well combined. Cover and refrigerate for at least 2 hours or until next day. Makes 2 cups.

Artichoke Hearts Vinaigrette

Cooked artichoke hearts topped with a tart dressing are featured in this versatile dish.

    Simmered Artichoke Hearts (page 73)
⅓ **cup olive oil or salad oil**
2 **tablespoons white wine vinegar**
½ **teaspoon dry mustard**
⅛ **teaspoon coarsely ground pepper**
2 **tablespoons chopped chives**
6 **hard-cooked eggs**
12 **cherry tomatoes**
6 **small inner celery stalks**
12 **Niçoise or ripe olives**

Prepare Simmered Artichoke Hearts. Let cool; then cover and refrigerate in cooking broth for at least 2 hours or until next day.

In a small bowl, mix oil, vinegar, mustard, and pepper until blended; set aside. Lift artichokes from broth and arrange on 6 individual plates. Sprinkle with chives. Cut eggs in half; arrange around artichokes, along with tomatoes, celery, and olives. Pour dressing over all. Makes 6 servings.

Artichokes with Mayonnaise

Fill whole artichokes with a piquant mayonnaise for an appealing first course. Another time, serve the zesty sauce as a dip for raw vegetables.

6 **medium to large artichokes**
1 **egg**
1½ **tablespoons *each* lemon juice and white wine vinegar**
1 **teaspoon Dijon mustard**
1 **clove garlic, minced or pressed**
6 **anchovy fillets, coarsely chopped**
1 **teaspoon grated lemon peel**
1 **cup salad oil**
3 **tablespoons chopped parsley**
1 **tablespoon capers, drained well**

Boil artichokes as directed on page 16. Drain and immediately plunge into cold water; drain again and place on paper towels. Pull out small pale center leaves and scoop out fuzzy choke; discard

inner leaves and choke. Cover artichokes and refrigerate until well chilled.

Place egg, lemon juice, vinegar, mustard, garlic, anchovies, and lemon peel in a blender or food processor. Whirl until blended. With motor on high, add oil, a few drops at a time at first, increasing to a slow, steady stream about ¹⁄₁₆ inch wide as mixture begins to thicken. (The slower the addition of oil, the thicker the sauce will be.) Add parsley and capers; whirl just until blended. Cover and refrigerate for at least 1 day or up to 1 week.

Spoon sauce evenly into centers of cold artichokes; dip leaves into sauce. Makes 6 servings.

Asparagus Victor

Stately asparagus spears stand in for celery in this version of the famous salad originated by Chef Victor Hirtzler of San Francisco's St. Francis Hotel.

2 **pounds asparagus**
1 **can (14½ oz.) regular-strength chicken broth**
6 **tablespoons olive oil or salad oil**
¼ **cup white wine vinegar**
2 **tablespoons *each* finely chopped green onion (including top) and pimento**
1 **teaspoon Dijon mustard**
¼ **teaspoon salt**
⅛ **teaspoon pepper**
  Shredded iceberg lettuce
2 **hard-cooked eggs**
  Cherry tomatoes
  Pitted ripe olives
1 **can (2 oz.) anchovy fillets (optional)**

Snap off and discard tough ends of asparagus; peel stalks, if desired. Boil asparagus according to directions on page 16, but substitute chicken broth for water. With tongs, transfer asparagus to a deep bowl. Reserve broth for other uses, if desired.

Stir together oil, vinegar, onion, pimento, mustard, salt, and pepper. Pour dressing over asparagus, cover, and refrigerate for 4 to 6 hours.

Just before serving, arrange a bed of lettuce on each of 4 to 6 individual plates. Lift asparagus from bowl and divide evenly among plates. Cut eggs into quarters and tomatoes in half; use to garnish each serving, along with olives and, if desired, anchovies. Drizzle remaining dressing over all. Makes 4 to 6 servings.

Asparagus in Belgian Endive

Pictured on page 34

Here's an elegant appetizer to show off the first asparagus of early spring, while Belgian endive is still in season. If endive isn't available, you can substitute small inner romaine leaves.

- 24 asparagus spears
- 24 large outer Belgian endive leaves (about 3 heads *total*) or small inner romaine leaves (about 2 heads *total*)
- ¼ cup olive oil or salad oil
- 2 tablespoons white wine vinegar
- 2 teaspoons Dijon mustard
   Chopped parsley

Snap off and discard tough ends of asparagus. Peel stalks, if desired. Cut tips to the same length as endive leaves; reserve remaining tender sections of asparagus for other uses.

Boil asparagus as directed on page 16. Drain and plunge immediately into cold water; when cool, place on a cloth and let drain.

In a small bowl, whisk oil, vinegar, and mustard until blended. Pour into a small serving bowl; top with parsley.

Place an asparagus spear in each endive leaf; offer on a serving tray with bowl of mustard sauce for dipping. If made ahead, cover and refrigerate for up to 6 hours. Makes 24 appetizers.

Celery Root & Green Beans

Celery root's tough, knobby exterior conceals a tender, creamy white interior with a celerylike flavor. For a first course, pair cooked celery root with green beans and toss with an anchovy dressing.

- ¼ cup white (distilled) vinegar
- 1½ cups water
- 1½ to 1¾ pounds celery root
- ¼ pound green beans
   Anchovy Dressing (recipe follows)
- 12 thin slices salami (optional)

Pour vinegar and 1 cup of the water into a 3 to 4-quart pan. Peel celery root and cut into ½-inch cubes. Drop immediately into pan. Bring to a boil over high heat; then reduce heat and simmer, uncovered, just until root is tender when pierced (about 10 minutes). Drain. (At this point, you may cool, cover, and refrigerate until next day.)

Cut beans lengthwise into thin strands. In a wide frying pan, bring remaining ½ cup water to a boil over high heat; add beans and cook, uncovered, until bright green and tender-crisp to bite (about 4 minutes). Drain and plunge immediately into cold water; drain again. (At this point, you may cool, cover, and refrigerate until next day.)

Prepare Anchovy Dressing. Mix with celery root and beans; mound on 4 individual plates. If desired, garnish with salami. Makes 4 servings.

Anchovy Dressing. In a small bowl, stir together ⅓ cup **salad oil;** 1½ tablespoons **white wine vinegar;** 5 canned **anchovy fillets** (chopped); ¾ teaspoon **thyme leaves;** and ⅛ teaspoon **pepper.**

Wilted Greens with Sausage

For a bit of showmanship, prepare the dressing at the table in a fondue pot or chafing dish; then toss with greens and serve immediately.

- 1 medium-size head escarole, chicory, or romaine
- ½ teaspoon sugar
- ¼ teaspoon dry mustard
- ⅛ teaspoon pepper
- 2 tablespoons red wine vinegar
- 3 strips bacon, cut into ¾-inch pieces
- 1 Polish sausage (6 to 8 oz.), thinly sliced

Clean and prepare greens as directed on page 8; you should have 6 cups bite-size pieces. Place in a plastic bag and refrigerate until serving time.

In a small bowl, combine sugar, mustard, pepper, and vinegar; set aside.

In a wide frying pan (or in a fondue pot or chafing dish) over medium heat, cook bacon until partially cooked; add sausage and cook until meats are browned. Discard all but 3 tablespoons of the drippings. (At this point, you may set aside for up to 2 hours. Reheat before continuing.)

Arrange greens in a large serving bowl. Place pan over low heat, add vinegar mixture, and cook, stirring, until blended and heated through. Pour dressing over greens and mix until greens are wilted. Serve immediately. Makes 4 servings.

Onion Knots with Peanut Sauce

Pictured on facing page

After a brief blanching in boiling water, green onions are pliable enough to be tied into knots.

  2 **to 3 dozen green onions (including tops)**
12 **cups water**
   Peanut Sauce (recipe follows)

Rinse onions and cut off roots. In a 5 to 6-quart kettle over high heat, bring water to a boil. Add onions, a few at a time, and cook just until green ends appear limp (about 20 seconds). Lift out and plunge immediately into cold water; when cool, place onions on a cloth and let drain.

Pull off and discard tough outside layers of each onion. Tie each onion in a loose knot so that white end protrudes about 1 inch; trim green end about 1 inch from knot. (At this point, you may cool, cover, and refrigerate for up to 6 hours.)

Prepare Peanut Sauce. Arrange onions on a tray; dip white ends into sauce. Makes 2 to 3 dozen appetizers.

Peanut Sauce. In a small bowl, combine ¼ cup *each* **crunchy peanut butter** and **plum jam,** 1 tablespoon *each* **lemon juice** and **soy sauce,** and **liquid hot pepper seasoning** to taste.

Parsnips with Crackling Pork

This first-course salad requires young, tender parsnips; don't use those with hard, woody cores.

   Crackling Pork (recipe follows)
¾ **pound parsnips, peeled**
 1 **cup *each* water and white (distilled) vinegar**
   Butter lettuce leaves
 1 **small red apple**

Prepare Crackling Pork.

Cut parsnips lengthwise into ¼-inch julienne strips. In a wide frying pan over high heat, bring water and vinegar to a boil. Add parsnips and boil gently, uncovered, just until tender-crisp to bite (about 5 minutes); drain well. If made ahead, cool, cover, and refrigerate until next day.

Line 4 individual plates with lettuce leaves; mound parsnips in center. Core and thinly slice apple, and arrange around parsnips. Spoon pork over parsnips. Makes 4 servings.

Crackling Pork. Finely dice ½ pound boneless **pork shoulder,** including fat. Place in a wide frying pan over low heat and cook, stirring occasionally, until crisp (about 35 minutes). Add 3 tablespoons **lemon juice,** 2 tablespoons **soy sauce,** 2 teaspoons **honey,** and 1 large clove **garlic** (minced or pressed). Continue to cook, stirring to free browned particles, until mixture comes to a boil.

If made ahead, let cool, cover, and refrigerate until next day. Reheat just before serving.

Chilled Leeks & Shrimp

This elegant, eye-catching first course is surprisingly simple to make. Prepare the leeks and the mustard dressing in advance; then assemble with romaine leaves and shrimp just before serving.

  6 **to 8 leeks, *each* about 1 inch in diameter**
½ **cup whipping cream**
¾ **cup mayonnaise**
1½ **tablespoons lemon juice**
 3 **tablespoons Dijon mustard**
   Salt and pepper
 6 **to 8 romaine leaves**
¾ **to 1 pound small cooked shrimp**

Prepare leeks as directed on page 10. Place in a single layer in a wide frying pan; add water to cover. (If pan won't hold all the leeks at once, cook in 2 batches.) Bring water to a boil over high heat; cover, reduce heat, and simmer until stem ends are tender when pierced (5 to 7 minutes). Lift out leeks; let cool, cover, and refrigerate until next day.

In a small bowl, beat cream until soft peaks form. Combine mayonnaise, lemon juice, and mustard; fold in cream, and season to taste with salt and pepper. (At this point, you may cover and refrigerate for up to 6 hours.)

Just before serving, arrange romaine leaves on 6 to 8 individual plates. Place 2 leek halves on each leaf and distribute shrimp evenly over leeks. Pass dressing at the table. Makes 6 to 8 servings.

FINGERS ALLOWED for dipping Asparagus in Belgian Endive (recipe on page 33) and tomatoes into vinaigrette, Onion Knots into spicy Peanut Sauce (recipe on this page).

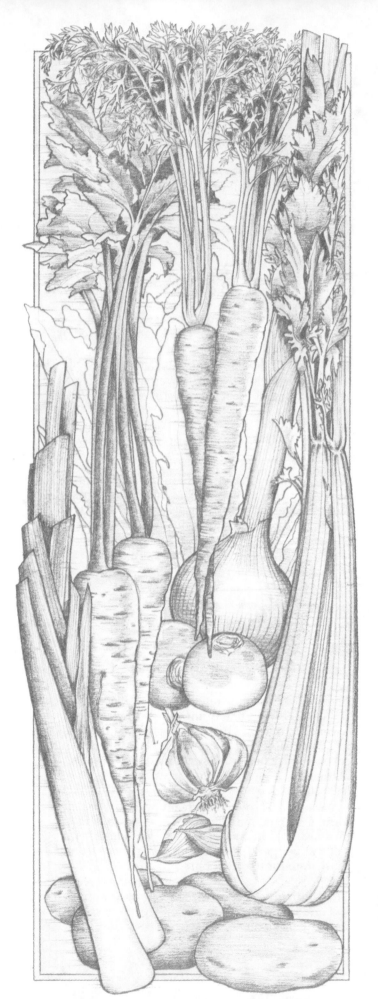

Soups

More likely than not, if you see a soup kettle simmering away, its contents include a healthy crop of fresh vegetables. And, be it a simple broth or a sophisticated purée, there's a vegetable soup for every occasion and every season—from a light, fresh dinner starter to a hearty entrée; from a warming lunch on a chilly day to a refreshing cooler on a hot one.

If you're serving soup as a first course, offer about one cup per serving. Serve heartier soups, such as cheese-sprinkled, chunky minestrone, in more generous portions for lunch or dinner.

ROOTS ARE FOR SOUPS! A selection of vegetables often found in the soup kettle: leeks, parsnips, carrots, onion, turnips, garlic, white thin-skinned potatoes, celery.

Daikon Soup

Serve this simple, clear soup to begin an Oriental meal. If daikon isn't available, substitute small turnips.

- 4 cups regular-strength beef broth
- 1 clove garlic, minced or pressed
- 2 teaspoons soy sauce
- 1 teaspoon sesame oil (optional)
- 2 cups thinly sliced peeled daikon or turnips (6 to 8 oz.)
  Thinly sliced green onions (including tops)

In a 3-quart pan over high heat, combine broth, garlic, soy, and, if desired, oil. Bring to a boil; then add daikon. Cover, reduce heat, and simmer until daikon is tender to bite (10 to 15 minutes). Garnish individual servings with onions. Makes about 6 cups.

Party Onion Soup

This soup's many virtues make it a perfect choice for casual entertaining: it's easy to make in quantity, it can be prepared ahead, and it stays warm over low heat for several hours—ready to serve drop-in guests.

- ½ cup (¼ lb.) butter or margarine
- 10 large onions (about 2½ lbs. *total*), thinly sliced
- ¼ cup all-purpose flour
- 8 cans (14½ oz. *each*) regular-strength beef broth
- 1 cup dry white wine (or ¼ cup lemon juice plus ¾ cup water)
  Salt and pepper
- 2 cups (8 oz.) shredded Gruyère or Swiss cheese
- 3 cups seasoned croutons

Melt butter in a 6 to 8-quart kettle over medium-high heat. Add onions; cover and cook, stirring occasionally, until soft (about 10 minutes). Uncover and continue to cook, stirring often, until onions are lightly browned (20 to 25 more minutes). If necessary, reduce heat toward end of cooking to prevent scorching.

Sprinkle flour over onions; cook, stirring, for about 1 minute. Remove from heat and gradually stir in 4 cans of the broth. Place kettle over high heat; add wine and bring to a boil, stirring. Cover, reduce heat, and simmer for 30 to 40 minutes. (At this point, you may cool, cover, and refrigerate for up to 2 days.)

Add remaining 4 cans broth and reheat slowly until very hot. Season to taste with salt and pepper. Sprinkle individual servings with cheese and croutons. Makes about 22 cups.

Mellow Mushroom Soup

Mushroom purée gains a special richness from the last-minute addition of egg and sour cream in this subtly flavored first-course soup. Contrast the soup's creamy texture with crunchy bread sticks or crusty French bread.

- 3 tablespoons butter or margarine
- 1 pound mushrooms, sliced
- 1 small onion, chopped
- 1 clove garlic, minced or pressed
- 1 teaspoon paprika
- ¼ cup all-purpose flour
- ½ teaspoon dry chervil
- 1 large can (49½ oz.) regular-strength chicken broth
- 1 egg
- ½ cup sour cream

Melt butter in a 5-quart kettle over medium-high heat. Add mushrooms, onion, and garlic, and cook, stirring often, until vegetables are lightly browned and all liquid has evaporated. Lift out about 12 mushroom slices and set them aside. Add paprika, flour, and chervil to kettle, and stir in. Cook, stirring, until bubbly. Gradually pour in broth and cook, stirring constantly, until soup is bubbly and thickened.

In a blender or food processor, whirl soup, a portion at a time, until smooth. (At this point, you may cool, cover, and refrigerate until next day.)

Just before serving, heat soup in kettle over medium heat until steaming. Meanwhile, in a soup tureen, beat egg lightly; then add sour cream and beat until blended. Slowly pour in hot soup, stirring constantly. Garnish soup in tureen with reserved mushroom slices. Makes about 8 cups.

Potato Bisque with Mustard Greens

Zesty mustard greens add a pleasant tang to this creamy bisque. Squeeze lemon wedges into each serving to accent the keen taste of the greens.

- 4 **tablespoons butter or margarine**
- 1 **large onion, chopped**
- 3 **quarts lightly packed mustard green leaves, cut into 1-inch strips**
- 3 **large russet potatoes, peeled and sliced**
- 4 **cups regular-strength chicken broth**
- 3 **cups milk**
- 1 **clove garlic, minced or pressed**
- ½ **cup whipping cream**
- ¼ **teaspoon ground nutmeg**
  Salt and pepper
  Lemon wedges
- 2 **hard-cooked eggs, finely chopped**

Melt butter in a 5 to 6-quart kettle over medium heat; add onion and cook until soft. Add greens and cook, stirring, until wilted. Add potatoes, broth, milk, and garlic; cover and simmer until potatoes are tender when pierced (25 minutes).

In a blender or food processor, whirl soup, a portion at a time, until smooth. Return to kettle; stir in cream and nutmeg and heat to simmering, stirring. Season to taste with salt and pepper. Pass lemon wedges to squeeze into individual servings and eggs to sprinkle on top. Makes 10 to 12 cups.

Watercress-Lemon Soup

Fresh watercress lends vibrant green color and piquancy to this smooth soup. For the tangiest flavor, use the full amount of lemon juice.

- 2 **cans (14½ oz. *each*) regular-strength chicken broth**
- 2 **small thin-skinned potatoes, cubed**
- ½ **cup milk**
- ½ **teaspoon ground nutmeg**
- 2 **tablespoons cornstarch**
- 4 **cups lightly packed watercress leaves**
- 2 to 3 **tablespoons lemon juice**
  Lemon slices (optional)
  Watercress sprigs (optional)

In a 4 to 5-quart kettle over high heat, combine broth and potatoes. Bring to a boil; then cover, reduce heat, and simmer until potatoes are very tender when pierced (about 15 minutes).

In a small bowl, mix milk, nutmeg, and cornstarch until smooth. Stir into potatoes and cook, stirring, until bubbly and thickened. Add watercress leaves and cook over medium heat just until leaves are wilted (about 1 minute). Remove from heat.

In a blender or food processor, whirl soup, a portion at a time, until smooth. (If using a blender, whirl first on low speed, then on high.) Return to kettle over high heat; bring to steaming, stirring constantly. Stir in lemon juice. Garnish individual servings with lemon slices and watercress sprigs, if desired. Makes about 6 cups.

Spring Garden Soup

Pictured on facing page

Thick with fresh spring vegetables, this colorful soup is an ideal beginning for a casual dinner party. For an easy meal, fill out the menu with bread, assorted cheeses, and cold sliced meats.

- 4 **tablespoons butter or margarine** *2T*
- 2 **cups diced carrots** *+ mushrooms sliced* *1 C*
- 1 **large can (49½ oz.) regular-strength chicken broth** *2 cans*
- 2 **cups thinly sliced asparagus (about ¾ lb.)** *1 C*
- ½ **cup thinly sliced green onions (including tops)** *red onion* *¼ C*
- 1 to 2 **cups shelled green peas or 1 package (10 oz.) frozen peas, thawed** *1 C*
- ¼ **cup minced parsley** *⅛ C*
  Salt and pepper

Melt butter in a 5-quart kettle over medium-low heat. Add carrots and cook, uncovered, stirring often, until tender-crisp to bite (5 to 7 minutes). Pour in broth and bring to a boil over high heat. Add asparagus, onions, and peas. Cover, reduce heat to medium-low, and simmer until asparagus is tender to bite (about 5 minutes). Stir in parsley and season to taste with salt and pepper. Makes 9 to 10 cups.

SALUTE THE SEASON with a potful of Spring Garden Soup (recipe on this page). Simmering broth brims with fresh asparagus, green peas, carrots, green onions.

Creamy Carrot Soup

Carrots lend a subtle sweetness to this quick-to-prepare cream soup that is ideal for a first course or a light lunch.

    2 tablespoons butter or margarine
    1 large onion, finely chopped
    3 cups finely chopped carrots
    2 tablespoons *each* tomato paste and rice
    4 cups regular-strength chicken broth
    ½ cup whipping cream
      Salt and pepper
      Parsley sprigs or carrot curls

Melt butter in a 3 to 4-quart pan over medium heat; add onion and cook, stirring often, until soft. Add carrots, tomato paste, rice, and broth. Bring to a boil; then cover, reduce heat, and simmer until carrots are very tender to bite (about 20 minutes).

In a blender or food processor, whirl about half the soup at a time until smooth. (At this point, you may cool, cover, and refrigerate for up to 2 days.)

Return soup to pan over medium heat; add cream and bring to simmering, stirring often. Season to taste with salt and pepper; garnish with parsley sprigs. Makes about 8 cups.

Tomato-Basil Soup

Nothing accents the sweetness of a ripe tomato better than the pungent flavor of fresh basil.

    3 tablespoons butter or margarine
    1 large onion, sliced
    1 large carrot, shredded
    4 large ripe tomatoes, peeled, seeded, and
      coarsely chopped (about 4 cups)
    ½ cup lightly packed fresh basil leaves or
      2 teaspoons dry basil
    ¾ teaspoon sugar
    ⅛ teaspoon white pepper
    1 can (14½ oz.) regular-strength chicken
      broth
      Salt
      Fresh basil leaves or minced parsley

Melt butter in a 3-quart pan over medium heat. Add onion and carrot; cook, stirring often, until

onion is soft. Stir in tomatoes, the ½ cup basil leaves, sugar, and pepper. Bring to a boil, stirring to prevent sticking; then cover, reduce heat, and simmer until onion is very soft (10 to 15 minutes).

In a blender or food processor, whirl soup, a portion at a time, until smooth. (At this point, you may cool, cover, and refrigerate until next day.)

Return tomato mixture to pan over medium heat; add broth and season to taste with salt. Heat until steaming. Garnish individual servings with basil leaves. Makes about 6 cups.

Cranberry Bean Minestrone

Fresh cranberry beans appear briefly in produce markets in mid-to-late summer; when they aren't available, substitute fresh or frozen lima beans.

    1½ pounds meaty beef shanks
      1 *each* carrot, onion, and celery stalk,
        cut up
      ¼ teaspoon pepper
    3½ quarts water
      2 large tomatoes, peeled and chopped
      3 small thin-skinned potatoes, sliced
      2 cups shelled cranberry or lima beans
        (about 1¼ lbs.) or 1 package (10 oz.)
        frozen lima beans, thawed
      ¼ cup pasta stars or other small macaroni
     12 Italian beans, cut into 1-inch pieces
      2 medium-size zucchini, sliced
      2 leeks (white parts only), sliced
    1½ cups shelled green peas (about 1½ lbs.
        unshelled) or 1 package (10 oz.) frozen
        peas, thawed
      2 teaspoons sugar
      ½ teaspoon dry basil
        Salt
        Grated Parmesan cheese

In an 8-quart kettle over high heat, place beef shanks, carrot, onion, celery, pepper, and water. Bring to a boil; then cover, reduce heat, and simmer until meat is very tender when pierced (about 2½ hours). Let cool slightly, then strain stock. Remove meat from bones. Discard bones and vegetables; cut meat into bite-size pieces and set aside.

Return strained stock to kettle over high heat; add tomatoes, potatoes, cranberry beans, and pasta. Bring to a boil; then cover, reduce heat, and simmer for 20 minutes. Add Italian beans, zuc-

chini, leeks, peas (if using frozen peas, add during last 5 minutes of cooking), sugar, basil, and reserved meat. Simmer for 10 more minutes; season to taste with salt. Pass cheese to sprinkle on individual servings. Makes about 24 cups.

Spring Greens & Ham Soup

Leafy spring greens and smoked ham hocks combine to make a hearty and colorful soup. Serve cornbread for a homey accompaniment.

    3   large meaty ham hocks, split (about 3 lbs. *total*)
    1   large clove garlic, minced or pressed
    2   small dried whole hot red chiles, crushed
    2½ quarts lightly packed greens, torn into bite-size pieces (choose at least 2 of the following: green or napa cabbage, dandelion greens, kale, mustard greens, spinach, Swiss chard)
    1   or 2 chicken bouillon cubes or 1 to 2 teaspoons chicken-flavored stock base
        Freshly ground pepper

Place ham hocks in a 5-quart kettle; cover with 2 quarts water and bring to a boil over high heat. Taste water; if salty, drain ham hocks, cover with 2 more quarts water and bring to a boil. If water still tastes salty, repeat with 2 more quarts water. Stir in garlic and chiles; then cover, reduce heat, and simmer until meat comes away from bones easily (about 2½ hours). Let cool; then strain stock. Cut meat into bite-size pieces and return to stock; discard bones and fat. (At this point, you may cool, cover, and refrigerate until next day.)

Skim (or lift off) and discard fat from stock. Bring to a boil over high heat; stir in greens and cook, uncovered, until greens are just tender to bite (about 5 minutes). Season to taste with bouillon cubes and pepper. Makes about 12 cups.

Bean & Vegetable Soup

On a chilly day, serve a lunch of salad, whole-grain bread, and this hearty Dutch soup—a savory combination of nut-sweet celery root, tender white beans, and Brussels sprouts simmered in beef broth.

    2   tablespoons salad oil
    1   medium-size onion, chopped
    ½   cup all-purpose flour
    3½ cans (14½ oz. *each*) regular-strength beef broth
    1   medium-size celery root (about 1 lb.), peeled and cut into ½-inch cubes
    3   cups cooked or 2 cans (about 16 oz. *each*) Great Northern beans, drained
    2   medium-size carrots, thinly sliced
    ¾   pound Brussels sprouts, halved lengthwise
    ½   cup whipping cream

Heat oil in a 6 to 8-quart kettle over medium-high heat; add onion and cook, stirring, until soft (about 5 minutes). Stir in flour; cook until bubbly. Gradually stir in broth, and cook, stirring, until mixture boils. Add celery root, beans, and carrots. Return to boil; then cover, reduce heat, and simmer until vegetables are tender when pierced (about 10 minutes). Add Brussels sprouts and cream and cook, uncovered, until sprouts are tender when pierced (about 10 more minutes). Makes about 14 cups.

Sparkling Gazpacho

Club soda contributes an effervescence that sets this gazpacho apart from others. To keep the bubbles lively, add the soda just before serving.

    1   can (12 oz.) tomato juice (1½ cups)
    4   medium-size tomatoes, peeled, seeded, and diced
    1   medium-size cucumber, peeled and diced
    ¼   cup *each* chopped green pepper and sliced green onions (including tops)
    1   small clove garlic, minced or pressed
    3   tablespoons *each* olive oil and red wine vinegar
    ½   teaspoon *each* chili powder and liquid hot pepper seasoning
        Dash of ground cloves
    1   bottle (10 oz.) club soda

Pour tomato juice into a large bowl. Add tomatoes, cucumber, green pepper, onions, garlic, oil, vinegar, chili powder, hot pepper seasoning, and cloves. Mix well; cover and refrigerate for at least 4 hours or until next day. Just before serving, stir soup well; then stir in soda. Makes about 6 cups.

Chilled Beet Soup

Pictured on facing page

Serve this pretty magenta soup chilled, with a topping of sour cream.

- 6 **cups peeled, diced beets (about 7 medium-size)**
- 2 **cans (14½ oz. *each*) regular-strength chicken broth**
- 2 **cups buttermilk**
- 1 **teaspoon dill weed**
- ¾ **cup thinly sliced green onions (including tops)**
  Salt and pepper
- 1 **large apple (optional)**
- 2 **teaspoons lemon juice (optional)**
  Sour cream

Combine beets and broth in a 3 to 4-quart pan over high heat. Bring to a boil; then cover, reduce heat, and simmer until beets are tender when pierced (about 25 minutes).

In a blender or food processor, whirl mixture, a portion at a time, until smooth. Stir in buttermilk, dill, and onions; season to taste with salt and pepper. Cover and refrigerate for at least 4 hours or until next day.

Pour into a serving bowl. Core and dice apple, if desired, and mix well with lemon juice. Pass apple and sour cream to spoon into individual servings. Makes 10 cups.

Curried Broccoli Soup

This cool, bright green soup, seasoned with curry, makes an inviting meal opener or lunchtime treat.

- 2 **pounds broccoli (about 2 bunches)**
- 2 **cans (14½ oz. *each*) regular-strength chicken broth**
- 3 **tablespoons butter or margarine**
- 2 **medium-size onions, chopped**
- 1½ **teaspoons curry powder**
  Sour cream
  Chopped salted peanuts

Cut tops of broccoli heads into small flowerets; then peel and thinly slice stalks. In a 3-quart pan over high heat, bring 1 cup of the broth to a boil. Add about half the flowerets; continue boiling, uncovered, until just tender when pierced (3 to 4 minutes). Drain, reserving broth. Let broccoli cool; then cover and refrigerate.

Melt butter in pan over medium heat. Add onions and cook, stirring often, until soft. Stir in curry powder and cook for 1 minute. Stir in broccoli stalks, uncooked flowerets, and all remaining broth. Cover and simmer until broccoli stalks are tender when pierced (about 12 minutes).

In a blender or food processor, whirl soup, a portion at a time, until smooth. Let cool; then cover and refrigerate for at least 4 hours or until next day. Top individual servings with reserved flowerets; pass sour cream and peanuts to spoon into soup. Makes 7 cups.

Cool Golden Chowder

This silky golden soup combines the summer's sweetest offerings: tender young carrots, crookneck squash, and corn freshly cut from the cob.

- 2 **tablespoons butter or margarine**
- 1 **medium-size onion, chopped**
- 1 **cup chopped carrots**
- 2½ **cups chopped crookneck squash**
- 1 **can (14½ oz.) regular-strength chicken broth**
- 1 **cup corn cut from cob (about 1 large ear)**
- ¼ **teaspoon thyme leaves**
  Salt and pepper
- ½ **cup milk**
  Chopped parsley
  Shelled sunflower seeds

Melt butter in a 3-quart pan over medium heat; add onion and cook, stirring often, until soft. Stir in carrots, squash, and broth; cover and simmer for 10 minutes. Add corn; cover and simmer until carrots are tender to bite (about 5 more minutes).

In a blender or food processor, whirl soup, a portion at a time, until smooth. Add thyme; season to taste with salt and pepper. Cover and refrigerate for at least 4 hours or until next day. Stir milk into cold soup; garnish with parsley. Pass seeds to sprinkle on individual servings. Makes 5 cups.

THIN SLICES of green onion bob atop ruby red Chilled Beet Soup (recipe on this page). Top with sour cream for a warm-weather version of Russian *borscht*.

Salads

*F*anciful, formal, tossed, or composed, salads adapt to any menu. Some introduce or accompany a meal; others satisfy as light entrées on those hot summer days when only something fresh and cool appeals to the appetite.

A salad can be an uncomplicated dish or a more elaborate one—a simple bowl of leafy greens tossed lightly with a traditional dressing, or an unusual combination of cooked vegetables attractively presented on a platter. Many of the salads in this chapter can be made ahead; they're ideal for picnics or buffets.

SPRIGHTLY GREENS for crisp, crunchy salads: mung bean sprouts, spinach, chicory (curly endive), romaine, leaf lettuce, butter lettuce, watercress, iceberg lettuce.

Marinated Cucumbers with Tomatoes

Try this no-fuss marinated salad as an accompaniment to barbecue fare or as part of an informal buffet.

2 tablespoons *each* sugar and white (distilled) vinegar
¼ teaspoon salt
2 medium-size cucumbers, peeled and thinly sliced
1 cup cherry tomatoes

In a bowl, combine sugar, vinegar, and salt; add cucumbers and mix well. Cover and refrigerate for 30 minutes to 1 hour, stirring occasionally.

Lift cucumbers from marinade and place in a serving dish. Cut tomatoes in half and arrange around cucumbers. Makes 6 to 8 servings.

Spring Asparagus Vinaigrette

Asparagus is one of the most lauded of seasonal specialties; each year, its arrival in the markets heralds the beginning of spring. The tender young spears are treated here to a double helping of dressing—first a simple marinade, then a creamy dill sauce to pass at the table.

2 pounds asparagus
⅓ cup sugar
½ cup salad oil
⅔ cup white wine vinegar
⅛ teaspoon *each* salt and pepper
½ medium-size onion, finely chopped
½ medium-size green pepper, seeded and finely chopped
Crisp romaine leaves
⅓ cup *each* sour cream and mayonnaise
⅛ teaspoon dill weed

Snap off and discard tough ends of asparagus; peel stalks, if desired. Boil as directed on page 16, cooking only until just tender when pierced (4 to 5 minutes).

Drain and plunge immediately into cold water;

when cool, drain again. Place in a shallow dish.

In a bowl, combine sugar, oil, vinegar, salt, pepper, onion, and green pepper; pour over asparagus. Cover and refrigerate for at least 4 hours or until next day.

Arrange romaine leaves on 6 individual plates. Lift asparagus from marinade; drain briefly (reserving 3 tablespoons of the marinade), then arrange on romaine leaves.

In a small bowl, combine sour cream, mayonnaise, dill, and reserved marinade. Pass at the table to spoon over individual servings of asparagus. Makes 6 servings.

Stuffed Lettuce

The dressing hides inside the lettuce in this unusual salad. Iceberg lettuce is filled with a vegetable-studded cream cheese mixture; when the head is cut into wedges, the dressing appears nestled in each piece.

¼ cup chopped almonds
1 large head iceberg lettuce
2 small packages (3 oz. *each*) cream cheese, softened
¼ cup mayonnaise or sour cream
1 tablespoon *each* prepared mustard and lemon juice
Liquid hot pepper seasoning
1 cup *each* finely chopped celery and shredded carrots
2 tablespoons *each* chopped green onion (including top), green pepper, and pimento
1 can (2¼ oz.) sliced ripe olives, drained

Spread almonds in a shallow pan and place in a 350° oven for about 8 minutes or until golden; set aside. Cut out and discard lettuce core, then hollow out a fist-size pocket to hold dressing. Reserve removed lettuce for other uses; set head aside.

In a bowl, combine cream cheese, mayonnaise, mustard, and lemon juice. Beat until well blended; season to taste with hot pepper seasoning. Stir in celery, carrots, onion, green pepper, pimento, olives, and almonds.

Fill lettuce pocket with dressing. Place stuffed lettuce, core side down, on a serving plate; cover with plastic wrap and refrigerate for 4 to 6 hours. Cut into wedges. Makes 6 servings.

Marinated Brussels Sprouts

The dwarf member of the cabbage family stars here in a versatile dish you can serve warm or chilled.

> About 1¼ pounds Brussels sprouts or 2 packages (10 oz. *each*) frozen Brussels sprouts
> ⅓ cup salad oil
> 3 tablespoons white wine vinegar
> 2 tablespoons thinly sliced green onion (including top)
> ¼ cup finely chopped ham, or 6 strips bacon, crisply cooked, drained, and crumbled
> 1 jar (2 oz.) sliced pimentos, drained
> ½ cup thinly sliced water chestnuts
> Salt and pepper

Cut fresh sprouts in half lengthwise. Boil as directed for whole Brussels sprouts on page 16, cooking only until just tender when pierced (about 7 minutes). Drain. (Or cook frozen sprouts according to package directions.)

Place sprouts in a serving bowl; add oil and vinegar and mix well. Stir in onion, ham, pimentos, and water chestnuts; season to taste with salt and pepper. Serve hot; or let cool, cover, and refrigerate until next day. Makes 4 to 6 servings.

Turnips with Mustard Greens

This combination of tender-crisp turnip strips and lightly wilted mustard greens is a warming salad for a chilly winter evening.

> 2 teaspoons sesame seeds
> 2 turnips, *each* about 2½ inches in diameter, peeled and cut into ⅛-inch julienne strips
> 3 tablespoons *each* white (distilled) vinegar, water, and sugar
> 3 tablespoons salad oil
> 4 cups lightly packed mustard greens
> 1 small red bell pepper, seeded and diced, or 1 jar (2 oz.) diced pimentos, drained

In a small frying pan over medium heat, toast sesame seeds, shaking pan frequently, until seeds are golden (about 2 minutes), then set aside.

In a wide frying pan, combine turnips, vinegar, water, and sugar. Cover and bring to a boil over high heat; continue boiling until turnips are tender-crisp to bite, about 3 minutes. (At this point, you may remove from heat, uncover, and let cool; then cover and refrigerate until next day. Reheat before continuing.)

Remove lid from pan and quickly stir in sesame seeds, oil, and mustard greens. Stir over medium heat just until greens are wilted. Pour into a shallow serving dish or 4 individual dishes and sprinkle with red pepper. Serve immediately. Makes 4 servings.

Rouge et Noir Salad

Pictured on facing page

Watercress is too good to be confined to the realm of garnishes—use it as a salad green, too. Here, the peppery sprigs make a piquant foil for bright red cherry tomato halves, sliced mushrooms, and glistening black olives.

> 2 bunches watercress
> ¾ pound mushrooms, sliced
> 1 can (3½ oz.) pitted ripe olives, drained
> 18 cherry tomatoes, halved
> 1 egg yolk
> ¼ cup lemon juice
> ½ teaspoon *each* sugar and dry basil
> ¼ teaspoon *each* salt and ground nutmeg
> ⅛ teaspoon white pepper
> ½ cup salad oil

Remove and discard tough stems from watercress. In a large bowl, combine watercress, mushrooms, olives, and tomatoes. Cover and refrigerate for 2 to 4 hours.

In a blender or food processor, combine egg yolk, lemon juice, sugar, basil, salt, nutmeg, and pepper; whirl until smooth. With motor running, slowly pour in oil and whirl until thickened. If made ahead, cover and refrigerate for 2 to 4 hours.

Arrange salad on 6 individual plates. Pass dressing at the table. Makes 6 servings.

BRIGHT red tomatoes and black olives highlight a tangle of tart watercress, all drizzled with creamy lemon dressing for Rouge et Noir Salad (recipe on this page).

Sunchoke Salad

Sunchokes, sometimes called Jerusalem artichokes, are the knotty brown roots of a plant related to the sunflower. They have a crunchy texture and a delicate, nutlike flavor—something like a potato.

In this hearty salad, steamed sunchokes are combined with celery, crisp bacon, and a flavorful mayonnaise dressing.

       2 cups water
       3 tablespoons lemon juice or white
          (distilled) vinegar
       1 pound sunchokes
       1 cup sliced celery
       ½ cup thinly sliced green onions
          (including tops)
       2 hard-cooked eggs, diced
       5 strips bacon, crisply cooked, drained,
          and crumbled
       ½ cup mayonnaise
       2 tablespoons sweet pickle relish, drained
       1 teaspoon Dijon mustard
          Salt and pepper
          Chopped parsley

In a medium-size bowl, combine water and lemon juice. Scrub sunchokes well; do not peel. Cut sunchokes crosswise into ¼-inch-thick slices and drop immediately into lemon water to prevent discoloration. Repeat until all are sliced, then lift from water and arrange on a steaming rack. Steam as directed on page 18, cooking only until just tender when pierced (5 to 7 minutes). Lift out and let cool.

In a large bowl, combine sunchokes, celery, onions, eggs, and bacon. In a measuring cup, stir together mayonnaise, relish, and mustard; stir into sunchoke mixture. Season to taste with salt and pepper. Cover and refrigerate for about 4 hours. Just before serving, stir again; then garnish with parsley. Makes 4 to 6 servings.

Caesar-style Vegetable Salad

A colorful assortment of raw vegetables stands in for romaine in this variation on the traditional Caesar salad.

       1 small bunch broccoli (about 1 lb.)
       1 small head cauliflower (about 1 lb.)
       1 small zucchini, thinly sliced
       2 large carrots, thinly sliced
       ¼ pound mushrooms, thinly sliced
       1 small green or red bell pepper, seeded
          and diced
          Caesar Dressing (recipe follows)
       1 egg
       ¾ cup grated Parmesan cheese

Cut flowerets off broccoli stalks; then cut flowerets into bite-size pieces. Trim and discard base of stalks; peel stalks and cut diagonally into thin slices. Cut cauliflower into bite-size pieces.

In a large bowl, combine broccoli, cauliflower, zucchini, carrots, mushrooms, and bell pepper. (At this point, you may cover and refrigerate for 4 to 6 hours.)

Prepare Caesar Dressing. In a small bowl, beat egg lightly; then mix with vegetables. Drizzle dressing over salad and sprinkle with cheese; mix well. Makes 6 to 8 servings.

Caesar Dressing. In a small bowl, stir together ¾ cup **olive oil** or salad oil, 6 tablespoons **lemon juice**, 2 cloves **garlic** (minced or pressed), 6 to 8 **anchovy fillets** (chopped), ¾ teaspoon **pepper**, and 1½ teaspoons **Worcestershire.**

Green Pea Salad

Fresh tomato wedges topped with sweet young peas make a colorful salad or vegetable side dish.

       1 to 1¼ cups shelled green peas (about 1¼
          lbs. unshelled) or 1 package (10 oz.)
          frozen peas, thawed
       ¼ cup *each* thinly sliced celery and green
          onions (including tops)
       ¼ cup shredded carrot
       1 tablespoon chopped parsley
       ¼ cup salad oil
       2 tablespoons white wine vinegar
       1 tablespoon catsup
       1 teaspoon sugar
       ¼ teaspoon *each* garlic salt, dry basil, and
          pepper
       4 medium-size tomatoes or 12 to 18 cherry
          tomatoes
          Butter lettuce cups

Boil fresh peas as directed on page 17 until tender to bite (5 to 10 minutes). Drain and plunge immediately into cold water; when cool, drain again.

In a small bowl, combine cooked (or thawed) peas, celery, onions, carrot, and parsley. In a measuring cup, stir together oil, vinegar, catsup, sugar, garlic salt, basil, and pepper. Pour dressing over pea mixture and stir well. Cover and refrigerate for 4 to 6 hours.

Remove and discard cores of tomatoes; then cut each into 6 wedges. Arrange each cut tomato in a lettuce cup so wedges resemble petals of a flower. Spoon salad evenly over tomatoes. (Or cut cherry tomatoes in half; spoon salad into lettuce cups and top with tomatoes.) Makes 4 servings.

Crunchy Potato Salad

Pictured on page 83

Crisp raw vegetables and chopped peanuts put crunch in this special potato salad.

> 2 **large white thin-skinned potatoes (about 1 lb.** *total***)**
> 6 **hard-cooked eggs, chopped**
> 1 **large green pepper, seeded and chopped**
> ½ **cup sliced green onions (including tops)**
> ⅔ **cup peeled, cubed jicama**
> 6 **to 8 radishes, sliced**
> **Sour Cream Dressing (recipe follows)**
> **Salt and pepper**
> **Green pepper rings, whole radishes, chopped salted peanuts**

Boil potatoes as directed on page 17 until tender when pierced (20 to 30 minutes); drain. When potatoes are cool enough to handle, peel them and cut into ½-inch cubes; you should have 2 to 3 cups. In a bowl, combine potatoes, eggs, green pepper, onions, jicama, and radishes.

Prepare Sour Cream Dressing and stir into potato mixture; season to taste with salt and pepper. Cover and chill for 2 to 4 hours. Garnish with pepper rings, radishes, and peanuts. Makes 6 servings.

Sour Cream Dressing. In a bowl, combine ½ cup **sour cream,** ¼ cup **mayonnaise,** ¼ cup drained **sweet pickle relish,** and 1 teaspoon **Dijon mustard.** Season to taste with **liquid hot pepper seasoning.**

Growing Sprouts in Your Kitchen

You don't need a green thumb—or even a garden—to grow sprouts. All you need is water and a container to keep the seeds moist.

Use tiny sprouts (alfalfa, chia, cress, mustard, and radish) to perk up salads and sandwiches, or try them tucked into an omelet. Larger sprouts (azuki, fenugreek, lentil, mung, rye, sunflower, and wheat) are delicious either raw or cooked; add them to stir-fried vegetable dishes for extra crunch.

Getting started. Most health food stores stock sprout seeds (sometimes packaged in mixes). You can also order seeds by mail from garden catalogues. Some seeds—lentils, sunflower seeds, and wheat berries—are available in supermarkets.

We've found that the best sprouting container is a 1 or 2-quart wide-mouth canning jar, placed on its side; replace the flat metal lid with cheesecloth or a purchased screen top.

Growing and harvesting. Use about 1 tablespoon alfalfa seeds or ¼ cup other seeds per quart. If you see broken and unhealthy seeds, discard them; then place seeds in the sprouting jar and soak overnight in 2 to 3 times their volume of water. Next morning, drain, rinse with lukewarm water, and drain again. While seeds are sprouting, rinse and drain several times daily to keep them moist. Seeds will begin to sprout in a day or two and finish within a week.

All sprouts need a warm place, but the need for light varies. Tiny sprouts need indirect sunlight to turn leaves green; harvest them when leaves open. Keep fenugreek and mung bean sprouts in a dark place. Azuki, lentil, rye, sunflower, and wheat sprouts grow in light or dark. Harvest large sprouts before leaves open or turn green.

Sprouts have best flavor and most nutrients if used soon after harvest. Any that aren't used immediately can be refrigerated in a plastic bag for up to one week.

Crisp Cabbage Slaw

For an informal barbecue or picnic, serve crunchy, horseradish-spiked coleslaw.

- 12 **cups shredded cabbage (green, red, or some of each)**
- ¾ **cup** *each* **sliced celery and green onions (including tops)**
- 1¼ **cups mayonnaise**
- 1 **tablespoon mustard seeds**
- 2 **teaspoons** *each* **prepared horseradish and Worcestershire**
- 3 **tablespoons sweet pickle relish, drained**
  Salt and pepper

In a large bowl, mix cabbage, celery, and onions. In another bowl, stir together mayonnaise, mustard seeds, horseradish, Worcestershire, and relish. Spoon dressing over cabbage mixture and mix well. Season to taste with salt and pepper. If made ahead, cover and refrigerate for 4 to 6 hours. Makes 8 to 10 servings.

Beet & Beet Green Salad

Mix sliced beets—the sweetest of the root vegetables—with an herbed vinaigrette; then top with fresh beet greens, butter-steamed to bring out their peppery-sweet flavor.

- ¼ **cup olive oil or salad oil**
- 2 **tablespoons red wine vinegar**
- 1 **clove garlic, minced or pressed**
- ½ **teaspoon** *each* **sugar and oregano leaves**
  Dash of pepper
- 4 or 5 **medium-size beets with tops**
  Salt
- 2 **tablespoons butter or margarine**
- 1 to 2 **tablespoons water**

In a measuring cup, combine oil, vinegar, garlic, sugar, oregano, and pepper. Mix well and set aside.

Trim beet tops 1 to 2 inches from crown and set

aside. Boil beets as directed on page 16, until tender throughout when pierced (30 to 40 minutes). Drain and let cool; then peel and cut into ¼-inch-thick slices. Mix beets with about half the dressing; season to taste with salt. Arrange beet slices on a serving platter and set aside.

Sliver beet tops. Place a wide frying pan or wok over high heat; when hot, add butter and greens. Cook, uncovered, stirring constantly, for 1 minute. Stir in water; cover and cook, stirring occasionally, until greens are lightly wilted (2 to 3 minutes). Remove from heat and mix with remaining dressing. Mound greens in center of beets on platter. Serve warm; or cover and refrigerate for at least 4 hours and serve cold. Makes 4 servings.

Spinach Salad with Bacon & Apples

Pictured on facing page

Crisp crumbled bacon, toasted almonds, and tart apples transform an ordinary spinach salad into something special.

- ⅓ **cup sliced almonds**
- 2 **large bunches spinach (about 1½ lbs. *total*)**
- 1 **large apple**
- 6 **strips bacon, crisply cooked, drained, and crumbled**
- 3 **tablespoons sliced green onions (including tops)**
- ½ **cup olive oil or salad oil**
- 6 **tablespoons tarragon wine vinegar or white wine vinegar**
- ¼ **teaspoon salt**
- 2 **teaspoons sugar**
- 1 **teaspoon dry mustard**
  Dash of pepper

Spread almonds in a shallow pan and toast in a 350° oven for about 8 minutes or until lightly browned; set aside. Prepare spinach as directed on page 12.

Tear spinach into bite-size pieces and place in a large serving bowl. Core and dice apple; add to spinach, along with almonds, bacon, and onions.

In a small bowl, combine oil, vinegar, salt, sugar, mustard, and pepper; mix well. Pour over salad and toss gently to coat. Makes 8 servings.

ALL THAT'S MISSING here is a big salad bowl for tossing the sweet, savory, and crisp ingredients of Spinach Salad with Bacon & Apples (recipe on this page).

Swedish-style Slaw

A tart vinegar dressing and mustard and celery seeds flavor this make-ahead salad. You can also serve it as a vegetable relish; or add a crunchy spoonful to a ham or corned beef sandwich.

> 1 medium-size head cabbage (about 2½ lbs.), finely shredded
> 1 teaspoon salt
> ¾ cup sugar
> ½ cup cider vinegar
> ¼ cup water
> 1 red or green bell pepper, seeded and thinly sliced
> 2 cups thinly sliced celery
> ½ cup thinly sliced green onions (including tops)
> 1 teaspoon *each* mustard seeds and celery seeds

In a large bowl, combine cabbage and salt; mix well and set aside.

Meanwhile, in a small pan over high heat, combine sugar, vinegar, and water. Bring to a boil and continue boiling, uncovered, for 1 minute. Remove from heat and let cool.

Add red pepper, celery, green onions, mustard seeds, and celery seeds to cabbage. Stir in cool syrup, mixing thoroughly. Cover and refrigerate for at least 6 hours or until next day.

Stir well; then lift cabbage mixture out of syrup, drain briefly, and spoon into a large serving bowl or individual bowls. Makes about 8 servings.

Fresh Corn Salad

Serve this tangy salad mounded on crisp lettuce leaves, or scoop spoonfuls into tomato cups.

> 4 ears corn, husks and silk removed
> Mustard-Caper Dressing (recipe follows)
> 3 hard-cooked eggs, finely chopped
> 1 cup finely diced celery
> 2 tablespoons *each* chopped green onion (including top), green pepper, and parsley
> Salt and pepper
> 6 crisp inner romaine or butter lettuce leaves

Boil corn as directed on page 17 until tender when pierced (3 to 5 minutes); drain. When corn is cool enough to handle, cut kernels from cob.

Prepare Mustard-Caper Dressing. In a large bowl, combine corn, eggs, celery, onion, green pepper, and parsley; stir in dressing and season to taste with salt and pepper. Cover and refrigerate for 2 to 4 hours. Spoon salad evenly into lettuce leaves. Makes 6 servings.

Mustard-Caper Dressing. In a small bowl, stir together ½ cup **mayonnaise**, 1 tablespoon *each* **Dijon mustard** and drained **capers**, 1 teaspoon **Worcestershire**, and 1 tablespoon **white wine vinegar**.

Festive Salad Bowl

Add color to a company dinner or a holiday buffet with this chunky vegetable salad. Prepare it ahead so vegetables can absorb the herb-flavored marinade.

> 1 pound green beans, cut diagonally into 2-inch pieces
> 1 can (6 to 8 oz.) water chestnuts, drained and sliced
> ½ pound mushrooms, sliced
> 1 can (8 oz.) pitted ripe olives, drained
> 16 to 18 cherry tomatoes, halved
> 2 jars (6 oz. *each*) marinated artichoke hearts
> ½ teaspoon dry basil
> ¼ teaspoon *each* oregano leaves and grated lemon peel
> 2 teaspoons lemon juice
> Garlic salt and pepper

Boil beans as directed on page 16 until tender-crisp to bite (4 to 7 minutes). Drain and plunge immediately into cold water; when cool, drain again. Place beans in a salad bowl.

Add water chestnuts and mushrooms to beans along with olives and tomatoes. Drain artichokes, reserving marinade; add artichokes (halved, if large) to bean mixture.

In a small bowl, combine reserved marinade, basil, oregano, lemon peel, and lemon juice; stir into vegetables. Season to taste with garlic salt and pepper. Cover and refrigerate for at least 4 hours or until next day. Makes 6 to 8 servings.

Whatever your preference in salad dressing—thick or thin, spicy or sweet—you'll find the perfect recipe here.

Mayonnaise

- 1 egg or 3 egg yolks
- 1 teaspoon Dijon mustard
- 1 tablespoon white wine vinegar or lemon juice
- 1 cup salad oil

In a blender or food processor, combine egg, mustard, and vinegar. Whirl until blended (about 4 seconds). With motor running, add oil, a few drops at a time at first, increasing to a slow, steady stream about 1/16-inch wide as mixture begins to thicken. (The slower the addition of oil, the thicker the sauce will be.) If made ahead, cover and refrigerate for up to 2 weeks. Makes 1½ cups.

Thousand Island Dressing. In a bowl, combine 1 cup **mayonnaise,** ¼ cup **tomato-based chili sauce,** 2 teaspoons minced **onion,** 1 tablespoon *each* minced **green pepper** and **pimento,** 2 tablespoons **sweet pickle relish,** and 1 **hard-cooked egg** (finely chopped). Season to taste with **salt** and **pepper.** Stir well. If desired, thin with a little **half-and-half** (light cream). If made ahead, cover and refrigerate for up to 1 week. Makes about 1½ cups.

Creamy Blue Cheese Dressing

- 1 pint (2 cups) sour cream
- 1 tablespoon lemon juice
- ½ teaspoon Worcestershire
- ⅛ teaspoon liquid hot pepper seasoning
- 1 clove garlic, minced or pressed
- 8 ounces blue-veined cheese or 6 ounces Roquefort, crumbled
  Pepper

In a bowl, combine sour cream, lemon juice, Worcestershire, hot pepper seasoning, and garlic; mix well. Stir in blue cheese, mashing any large pieces with a fork, until well blended. Season to taste with pepper. If made ahead, cover and refrigerate for up to 10 days. Makes about 2½ cups.

Vinaigrette Dressing

- 1 tablespoon finely chopped shallots or mild red onion
- 1 tablespoon Dijon mustard
- 3 tablespoons wine vinegar
- ½ cup olive oil or salad oil

In a small bowl or jar, combine shallots, mustard, vinegar, and oil; mix well. If made ahead, cover and refrigerate for up to 2 weeks. Makes ¾ cup.

Spicy French Dressing

- ½ cup sugar
- 1 tablespoon all-purpose flour
- ½ cup cider vinegar
- 1 teaspoon *each* salt and Worcestershire
- ½ cup finely chopped onion
- 1 clove garlic, minced or pressed
- 1 cup salad oil
- ⅓ cup catsup
- 1 teaspoon celery seeds

In a small pan, combine sugar, flour, and vinegar. Cook, stirring, over medium heat until bubbly and thickened; pour into a blender or food processor. Add salt, Worcestershire, onion, and garlic; whirl until smooth. With motor running, gradually add oil in a slow, steady stream until blended. Pour mixture into a bowl and stir in catsup and celery seeds. If made ahead, cover and refrigerate for up to 4 weeks. Makes about 2 cups.

Cumin Cabbage Slaw

Cumin adds a Latin accent to this coleslaw, which complements barbecued beef or pork.

- 8 **cups finely shredded green cabbage**
- 1 **cup finely shredded carrots**
- 6 to 8 **radishes, thinly sliced**
- ¼ **cup thinly sliced green onions (including tops)**
- ½ **cup** *each* **mayonnaise and sour cream**
- ½ **cup buttermilk**
- 1 **tablespoon** *each* **Dijon mustard and white wine vinegar**
- 2 **teaspoons cumin seeds**
  Salt and pepper

In a large bowl, combine cabbage, carrots, radishes, and onions. Set aside.

In a bowl, combine mayonnaise and sour cream; mix until smooth. Stir in buttermilk, mustard, vinegar, and cumin seeds. Stir dressing into salad; mix well and season to taste with salt and pepper. If made ahead, cover and refrigerate for 4 to 6 hours. Makes about 6 servings.

Stir-fry Vegetable Salad

Pictured on facing page

For a satisfying one-dish lunch, serve this Oriental-style salad. Crisp stir-fried vegetables and small shrimp are chilled in a soy-flavored marinade, then topped with crunchy cashews.

- ½ **pound broccoli**
- ½ **pound edible-pod peas**
- 2 **tablespoons salad oil**
- 2 **cloves garlic, minced or pressed**
- ¾ **teaspoon minced fresh ginger**
- ½ **pound mushrooms, thinly sliced**
- ⅓ **cup regular-strength chicken broth**
- 1 **tablespoon soy sauce**
- ½ **teaspoon sugar**
- 1 **tablespoon oyster sauce (optional)**
- 1 **can (4½ oz.) small shrimp, drained**
- 1 **jar (2 oz.) sliced pimentos, drained**
- ½ **cup mayonnaise (optional)**
  Crisp lettuce leaves
- ¼ **cup salted cashews or slivered almonds**

Cut flowerets off broccoli stalks; then cut flowerets into ¼-inch-thick slices. Trim and discard base of stalks; peel stalks and cut crosswise into ⅛-inch-thick slices. Remove and discard strings from peas. Set broccoli and peas aside.

Heat oil in a wok or wide frying pan over high heat; add garlic and ginger and cook, stirring, for 1 minute. Add broccoli, peas, and mushrooms; cook, stirring, until vegetables are just tender-crisp to bite (3 to 4 minutes). Pour into a bowl.

In a measuring cup, stir together broth, soy, sugar, and, if desired, oyster sauce. Pour over vegetables; then stir in shrimp and pimentos. Cool, cover, and refrigerate for at least 4 hours.

Drain vegetables, discarding liquid. If desired, stir in mayonnaise. Spoon over lettuce leaves and sprinkle with cashews. Makes 4 servings.

Bacon & Cauliflower Salad

Crisp bacon bits and snowy cauliflower, mixed with a creamy dressing and mounded atop shredded lettuce, make a hearty salad.

- **Creamy Dressing (recipe follows)**
- 1 **medium-size head cauliflower (about 1¼ lbs.)**
- 1 **small mild red onion, finely chopped**
- 1 **pound sliced bacon, crisply cooked, drained, and crumbled**
  Pepper
  Lettuce leaves
- 3 **cups shredded iceberg lettuce**

Prepare Creamy Dressing. Break cauliflower into flowerets and slice thinly. Place in a large bowl; add dressing, onion, and half the bacon. Season to taste with pepper. (At this point, you may cover and refrigerate until next day.) Line a salad bowl with lettuce leaves and mound shredded lettuce in center. Top with cauliflower mixture; sprinkle with remaining bacon. Makes 4 to 6 servings.

Creamy Dressing. In a bowl, stir together 1 cup **mayonnaise,** 3 tablespoons **lemon juice,** 1 tablespoon *each* **prepared mustard** and **dry basil,** and ⅛ teaspoon **ground nutmeg.**

FROM WOK TO MARINADE, crunchy Stir-fry Vegetable Salad (recipe on this page) garners flavors from the Orient. Hot tea and fried won tons make good go-alongs.

Entrées

M ore and more often, it seems, vegetables play a leading role in menu planning. To reflect that leap from supporting cast to star, we offer a collection of main dishes to show off the glory of seasonal bounty.

This chapter features vegetables in main-dish soups and stews, ideal to combat winter's chill, and in whole-meal salads, perfect for those summer days when you want a light yet satisfying entrée. Here, too, you'll find quick and delicious dishes for busy-night dinners, and interesting foreign entrées to star at dinner parties.

FRESH AND HEARTY vegetables to star in entrées: Swiss chard, bell peppers, cabbage, mushrooms, lentils and pinto beans, eggplant, cranberry beans, russet potatoes, spaghetti squash.

Special-occasion Salad Buffet

We've expanded the whole-meal salad idea and come up with a buffet that will serve 25 guests. For just a dozen or so, you can simply cut the recipe in half.

The dressing can be made four days ahead, and virtually everything else a day or two before the party.

Creamy Tarragon Dressing (recipe follows)
2 broiler-fryer chickens (about 3½ lbs. *each*)
1 canned ham (about 3 lbs.)
1 to 1½ pounds *each* Swiss cheese and sharp Cheddar cheese
1 large cauliflower (1½ to 2 lbs.)
2 large mild red onions, thinly sliced
1 pound carrots, thinly sliced
3 or 4 large zucchini, thinly sliced
4 large cucumbers, peeled and sliced
1½ pounds mushrooms, quartered
2 baskets cherry tomatoes
1 or 2 baskets alfalfa sprouts
2 large heads *each* iceberg, romaine, and red leaf lettuce
1 small head red cabbage, shredded

Prepare Creamy Tarragon Dressing.

Rinse chicken and pat dry; reserve giblets for other uses. Place chickens and ham on a rack in a large roasting pan. Bake in a 350° oven for about 1½ hours or until meat near chickens' thighbones is no longer pink when slashed. Let cool. Remove chicken meat from bones; discard skin and bones and tear meat into thin strips. Cut ham and cheeses into strips. Package meats and cheeses separately and refrigerate for up to 2 days.

Break cauliflower into flowerets; then cut into ¼-inch slices. Package cauliflower and other vegetables separately and refrigerate for up to 2 days.

Clean and prepare lettuce as directed on pages 10–11. Package with shredded cabbage and refrigerate until next day.

Serve buffet-style: Arrange meats, cheese, and vegetables in separate mounds on large boards or trays; place mixed greens in a large bowl. Pour dressing into 1 or 2 containers. Makes about 25 servings.

Creamy Tarragon Dressing. In a blender or food processor, combine ¾ cup **white wine vinegar,** 4 **egg yolks,** 2 tablespoons **dry tarragon,** 4 to 6 cloves **garlic** (minced or pressed), 2 teaspoons **salt,** and ½ teaspoon **pepper.** Whirl until blended. With motor running, slowly pour in 3 cups **salad oil** in a thin stream; continue whirling until mixture is thickened. Cover and refrigerate for up to 4 days. Makes 1 quart.

Taco Salad

Now you can enjoy tacos in neat-to-eat salad form. Combine traditional taco makings—crisp lettuce, juicy tomato, spicy meat, sharp cheese—in a bowl; add corn chips as a stand-in for taco shells. Prepared taco sauce and sour cream act as the dressing.

1 pound lean ground beef
1 large onion, chopped
1 tablespoon chili powder
½ teaspoon *each* ground cumin and oregano leaves
Prepared taco sauce
1 medium-size head iceberg lettuce, shredded
¼ pound bean sprouts
1 cup thinly sliced green onions (including tops)
1 small cucumber, peeled, seeded, and diced
1½ cups (6 oz.) shredded sharp Cheddar cheese
3 cups crushed tortilla or corn chips
2 medium-size tomatoes, cut into wedges
Sour cream

Crumble beef into a wide frying pan over medium-high heat; cook, stirring, until browned. Stir in onion and cook until soft; spoon off and discard excess fat. Add chili powder, cumin, oregano, and 2 to 3 tablespoons taco sauce; mix well and remove from heat.

Place lettuce in a large salad bowl. Add bean sprouts, green onions, cucumber, and cheese. Add meat mixture and tortilla chips; mix well. Garnish with tomatoes.

Pass sour cream and additional taco sauce at the table to spoon on individual servings. Makes 6 to 8 servings.

Vegetable Curry

You won't miss meat when you taste this satisfying curry. Spoon the spicy mixture of fresh vegetables and garbanzos over hot cooked rice and top with condiments; offer slices of melon for a cooling dessert.

> 6 tablespoons salad oil
> 1 large onion, thinly sliced
> 2 cloves garlic, minced or pressed
> 1 tablespoon minced fresh ginger
> 1 tablespoon curry powder
> ½ teaspoon *each* ground cumin and coriander
> ⅛ to ¼ teaspoon ground red pepper (cayenne)
> 2 large tomatoes, peeled and chopped
> ½ cup plain yogurt
> ½ pound mushrooms, sliced
> 1 large green pepper, seeded and cut into thin strips
> 2 medium-size carrots, thinly sliced
> 4 medium-size zucchini, cut into ½-inch thick slices
> 2 cans (about 1 lb. *each*) garbanzo beans, drained
> Salt
> 2 tablespoons chopped fresh coriander (cilantro) or parsley
> Hot cooked rice
> Condiments (suggestions follow)

Heat oil in a 5-quart kettle over medium-low heat. Add onion, garlic, and ginger; cook, stirring, until onion is soft. Add curry powder, cumin, coriander, red pepper, and tomatoes. Cook, stirring occasionally, until tomatoes are very soft (about 10 minutes). Stir in yogurt, mushrooms, green pepper, carrots, and zucchini. Bring to a boil over high heat; then cover, reduce heat, and simmer, stirring occasionally, until carrots are barely tender (about 10 minutes). Add garbanzos. Cover and simmer until garbanzos are heated through (about 5 minutes). Season to taste with salt.

Pour into a serving dish and sprinkle with coriander. Spoon over rice; top with condiments. Makes 4 to 6 servings.

Condiments. In separate bowls, place ½ cup **roasted peanuts**, ½ to 1 cup **plain yogurt** mixed with ½ to 1 tablespoon chopped **fresh coriander** or mint, and 3 or 4 chopped **hard-cooked eggs**.

Country Corn Omelet

Pictured on facing page

The toppings of this open-faced omelet are contrasts in flavors and texture: piquant greens, sweet corn, crisp bacon, crunchy almonds, and cool sour cream.

> 2 large ears corn, husks and silk removed
> 4 strips bacon, diced
> ¼ cup sliced almonds
> About 4 tablespoons butter or margarine
> 1 small onion, chopped
> 4 cups lightly packed coarsely shredded kale or Swiss chard
> 6 to 8 eggs
> ½ cup finely diced jack cheese
> ⅓ cup sour cream

With a sharp knife, cut corn kernels from cobs and set aside. In a wide frying pan over medium heat, cook bacon until crisp. Lift out, drain, and set aside. Add almonds to pan drippings. Cook, stirring gently, until lightly browned (1 to 2 minutes). Lift out and set aside.

Pour pan drippings into a measuring cup; add butter, if needed, to make ¼ cup. Return drippings and butter to pan; add corn and onion and cook over medium heat, stirring often, until onion is soft (about 6 minutes). Remove corn and onion from pan; keep warm.

Place kale and 1 tablespoon of the remaining butter in pan. Cook, stirring, until tender to bite (about 2 minutes); remove from pan and keep warm.

Reduce heat to medium-low and melt remaining 2 tablespoons butter in pan. In a bowl, beat eggs just until blended; pour into pan. When eggs begin to set, push cooked portion aside to allow uncooked eggs to flow underneath. When eggs are set but top still looks moist and creamy, remove from heat. Arrange kale evenly atop eggs; spoon corn mixture over kale, then sprinkle evenly with cheese and bacon. Mound sour cream in center; garnish with almonds. Present omelet in pan; cut into wedges to serve. Makes 4 servings.

SKILLET SUPPER features Country Corn Omelet (recipe on this page), with layers of vegetables topping creamy eggs. Crusty bread and white wine complete the menu.

Stuffed Bell Peppers Italiano

Pictured on front cover

A spicy scramble of sausage and summer vegetables bakes inside juicy bell peppers. For the sweetest flavor, use red bell peppers.

1 pound mild Italian sausage
1 large onion, chopped
2 cloves garlic, minced or pressed
1 large eggplant, cut into ½-inch cubes
1 large tomato, chopped
¼ pound mushrooms, sliced
1 teaspoon *each* thyme leaves, ground cumin, and crushed fennel seeds
8 large red or green bell peppers
½ cup chopped walnuts
1 egg
1 cup (4 oz.) shredded Cheddar cheese

Remove sausage casings; crumble meat into a wide frying pan over medium heat and cook until browned. Add onion and garlic and cook, stirring, until onion is soft. Stir in eggplant, tomato, mushrooms, thyme, cumin, and fennel seeds. Cook, uncovered, stirring occasionally, until eggplant is very tender to bite and liquid has evaporated (about 15 minutes). Let cool slightly.

Cut off pepper tops; remove seeds. Drop peppers and tops into a large quantity of boiling water; boil, uncovered, for 3 minutes. Drain, plunge into cold water, then drain again. Arrange peppers in a greased, shallow 2-quart baking dish. Stir walnuts, egg, and ½ cup of the cheese into vegetable mixture; evenly spoon into peppers. Replace pepper tops.

Bake, covered, in a 400° oven for 25 minutes or until hot throughout. Uncover, remove pepper tops, sprinkle filling with remaining ½ cup cheese, and bake for 10 more minutes or until cheese is melted. Replace tops, if desired. Makes 8 servings.

Lamb-Stuffed Cabbage Rolls

Freezing a whole head of cabbage is the best way to get the pliable leaves you need for making cabbage rolls—and it's much easier than the usual laborious technique of blanching individual leaves. These lamb-stuffed rolls are spicy with curry and chutney; a hint of cinnamon flavors the sauce.

1 large head cabbage (about 2½ lbs.), cored
3 tablespoons salad oil
1 medium-size onion, chopped
3 tablespoons *each* curry powder and coarsely chopped Major Grey's chutney
1 tablespoon vinegar
1 teaspoon *each* salt and ground coriander
½ teaspoon pepper
2 pounds lean ground lamb or ground beef
⅓ cup fine dry bread crumbs
1 egg
1 can (14½ oz.) regular-strength beef broth
1 or 2 whole cinnamon sticks, *each* 2 to 3 inches
3 tablespoons all-purpose flour
¼ cup water
Condiments (suggestions follow)

Several days ahead, wrap unwashed cabbage in foil and freeze. To thaw, unwrap and place in a bowl of lukewarm water for about 1 hour. To separate leaves, hold cabbage under warm running water and gently peel off one leaf at a time; you'll need 12 to 16 large leaves. (Reserve remaining cabbage to use in soup, if desired.) For easier rolling, trim off thick stem end of each leaf.

Heat oil in a small frying pan over medium heat; add onion and curry powder and cook, stirring, until onion is soft. In a bowl, combine chutney, vinegar, salt, coriander, pepper, lamb, bread crumbs, and egg; then mix in onion mixture.

Use about ½ cup of the meat mixture to fill larger leaves, a little less for smaller ones. Place meat near base of each leaf and roll leaf to enclose filling, tucking ends under. Place rolls, seam side down, in a 9 by 13-inch baking dish. (At this point, you may cover and refrigerate for up to 6 hours.)

Pour broth over cabbage rolls; add cinnamon sticks. Cover and bake in a 350° oven for 1¾ hours or until filling is no longer pink when slashed.

With a slotted spoon, transfer cabbage rolls to a platter; keep warm. Skim and discard fat from broth; pour broth into a pan. Mix flour and water until smooth; stir into broth. Cook, stirring, until sauce boils and thickens. Pass sauce to spoon on cabbage rolls, and 3 or more condiments to sprinkle atop. Makes 6 to 8 servings.

Condiments. In separate bowls, place **Major Grey's chutney,** coarsely chopped **apples** or **peanuts,** sliced **bananas,** sliced **green onions** (including tops), and **shredded coconut.**

Meat-stuffed Kohlrabi

What belongs to the cabbage family, tastes like a delicate turnip, and resembles neither vegetable? Answer: kohlrabi (the name means "cabbage-turnip" in German). Both the leaves and the above-ground bulb of this odd-looking vegetable are edible, and both are used here.

    6 to 8 large kohlrabi, *each* 2½ to 3 inches in diameter, with leaves and stems attached
    1 tablespoon salad oil
    1 small onion, chopped
    2 cloves garlic, minced or pressed
    ½ pound *each* ground veal and ground pork
    3 tablespoons fine dry bread crumbs
    1 egg
    ½ teaspoon salt
      Dash of pepper
    ⅛ teaspoon mace
    2 chicken bouillon cubes
    1½ cups boiling water
      Milk
    2 tablespoons butter or margarine
    2 tablespoons all-purpose flour

Cut kohlrabi leaves and stems from bulbs. Chop enough tender inner leaves to make 1 cup. Discard stems and remaining leaves. Peel and discard tough outer skin from bulbs; then scrape out center of each, leaving a ¼-inch-thick shell. Chop flesh, combine with leaves, and set aside.

Heat oil in a wide frying pan over medium heat. Add onion and garlic and cook, stirring, until onion is soft; transfer to a bowl and mix in veal, pork, bread crumbs, egg, salt, pepper, and mace. Fill kohlrabi shells with meat mixture and place in pan. Scatter chopped leaves and flesh in pan. Dissolve bouillon cubes in water and pour into pan. Bring to a boil over high heat; then cover, reduce heat, and simmer until kohlrabi shells are tender when pierced (about 50 minutes).

Transfer kohlrabi shells to a serving platter; keep warm. Strain pan liquid (discard leaves and flesh) and add enough milk to make 1¼ cups total; set aside. Melt butter in a pan over medium heat. Stir in flour and cook, stirring, until bubbly; gradually stir in milk mixture. Continue to cook, stirring, until sauce boils and thickens. Spoon over kohlrabi. Makes 4 servings.

South American Corn Pie

Creamy corn custard fills a vegetable-studded, spicy beef shell in *pastel de choclo*, a South American version of French *quiche*.

    4 tablespoons salad oil
    1 large onion, chopped
    ½ cup chopped green or red bell pepper
    1 medium-size tomato, peeled, seeded, and chopped
    2 cloves garlic, minced or pressed
    ½ cup *each* sliced pimento-stuffed green olives and raisins
    ¼ to ½ teaspoon crushed red pepper
    1 teaspoon *each* ground cumin and paprika
    1 pound lean ground beef
    ¼ cup fine dry bread crumbs
    1½ teaspoons salt
    2½ cups corn cut from cob (about 3 large ears) or part of a 1-pound package frozen corn, thawed
    ¼ cup sliced green onions (including tops)
    2 eggs
    ⅓ cup milk
    1 tablespoon all-purpose flour
    1 hard-cooked egg, sliced
      Fresh coriander (cilantro) sprigs

Heat 2 tablespoons of the oil in a wide frying pan over medium-high heat; add onion, green pepper, tomato, and garlic. Cook, stirring often, until vegetables are soft and tomato juice has evaporated (about 10 minutes). Stir in olives, raisins, red pepper, cumin, and paprika. Remove from heat.

In a bowl, combine beef, bread crumbs, and 1 teaspoon of the salt; add vegetable mixture and mix until well blended. Press over bottom and up sides to rim of a 10-inch pie pan or a 10-inch frying pan with ovenproof handle. Set aside.

Heat remaining 2 tablespoons oil in pan over medium heat; add corn and green onions. Cook, stirring often, for about 5 minutes. Spoon corn mixture evenly into meat shell. In a bowl, beat together eggs, milk, flour, and remaining ½ teaspoon salt; pour over corn. Bake, uncovered, in a 350° oven for 35 minutes or until center feels set when touched lightly. Let stand 10 minutes. Garnish pie with egg slices and coriander sprigs. Cut into wedges to serve. Makes 6 servings.

Onion-Zucchini Quiches

Pictured on facing page

Individual quiches laced with shredded zucchini, green onions, and Swiss cheese make great picnic fare to eat out of hand—or serve these tasty treats in their baking pans for a luncheon entrée.

   Buttery Pastry Dough (recipe follows)
1 cup lightly packed shredded zucchini
1 cup (4 oz.) shredded Swiss cheese
1 tablespoon all-purpose flour
½ cup finely chopped green onions (including tops)
3 eggs
1½ cups half-and-half (light cream)
1 clove garlic, minced or pressed
¼ teaspoon garlic salt
⅛ teaspoon pepper
24 or 30 thin slices zucchini, *each* 1 to 1¼ inches in diameter (1 or 2 small zucchini)

Prepare Buttery Pastry Dough. Divide dough evenly among eight 4-inch tart pans or ten 3-inch pans and press dough evenly over bottoms of pans and up sides to rims. Place pans on a large baking sheet.

In a bowl, combine shredded zucchini, cheese, and flour; toss to blend. Divide zucchini mixture equally among pastry shells; sprinkle with onions.

In another bowl, beat eggs, half-and-half, garlic, garlic salt, and pepper until blended. Divide equally among pastry shells (don't let mixture overflow or pastry will stick to pans). Arrange 3 zucchini slices, slightly overlapping, in center of each quiche.

Bake, uncovered, on lowest rack of a 350° oven for 35 to 40 minutes or until filling puffs and tops are lightly browned. Let stand for about 10 minutes (filling will settle). Protecting your hands, tip each quiche out of its pan into your hand and place on a rack, filling side up, to cool. If made ahead, let cool completely, cover, and refrigerate until next day.

Serve at room temperature; or place quiches side by side on a baking sheet and reheat, uncovered, in a 350° oven for 10 minutes. Makes eight 4-inch quiches or ten 3-inch quiches.

Buttery Pastry Dough. In a bowl, combine 1½ cups **all-purpose flour** and ¼ teaspoon **salt**. Cut 10 tablespoons (¼ lb. plus 2 tablespoons) **butter** or margarine into chunks and add to flour mixture. With two knives or a pastry blender, cut butter into flour mixture until it resembles fine crumbs. Add 1 **egg** and stir with a fork until dough holds together.

Stir-fried Beef with Bok Choy

When you have a wok, fresh-tasting dishes are easy to prepare in a hurry. One example: this mixture of thin steak strips and fresh bok choy in a gingery sauce.

   Cooking Sauce (recipe follows)
¾ pound lean boneless beef steak (such as sirloin, flank, or top round)
1 tablespoon soy sauce
1 medium-size head bok choy
4 tablespoons salad oil
1 clove garlic, minced or pressed
¼ cup water

Prepare Cooking Sauce; set aside.

Cut meat into thin 1 by 3-inch strips; place in a bowl and stir in soy. Set aside.

Cut bok choy leaves from stems. Cut stems diagonally into ¼-inch slices and coarsely shred leaves; you should have 6 to 8 cups lightly packed stems and leaves.

Heat a wok or wide frying pan over high heat. When hot, add 2 tablespoons of the oil, garlic, and bok choy stems. Cook, uncovered, stirring constantly, for 1 to 2 minutes. Add water, then cover and cook for 2 minutes; add leaves and cook, stirring occasionally, until just tender to bite (1 to 2 more minutes). Remove from wok.

Pour remaining 2 tablespoons oil into wok. When oil is hot, add meat; cook, stirring constantly, until meat is lightly browned (about 4 minutes). Stir Cooking Sauce; return bok choy to wok and add sauce. Cook, stirring, until sauce boils and thickens. Makes 2 to 3 servings.

Cooking Sauce. In a bowl, combine ¾ cup regular-strength **chicken broth**, 4 teaspoons **cornstarch**, 2 teaspoons **soy sauce**, 1 teaspoon minced **fresh ginger** or ½ teaspoon ground ginger, and 2 tablespoons **dry sherry.**

TREAT YOURSELF—and guests, if you like—to individual Onion-Zucchini Quiches (recipe on this page). Accompany with iced cider and a bunch of green grapes.

Fillet of Sole with Sorrel

Sorrel, though not widely used in American cooking, is a staple in French cuisine. Here, it complements lightly cooked sole fillets.

    4 tablespoons butter or margarine
 1½ to 2 pounds sole fillets
    ½ cup thinly sliced green onions
        (including tops)
    1 bottle (8 oz.) clam juice
    3 tablespoons lemon juice
    2 tablespoons all-purpose flour
    ⅔ cup milk
    ¼ teaspoon Dijon mustard
    ⅛ teaspoon ground nutmeg
    3 cups lightly packed finely shredded
        sorrel
        Lemon wedges

Melt 2 tablespoons of the butter in a wide frying pan over medium heat. Place fillets in pan; turn over to coat with butter, then arrange in an even layer and sprinkle with about half the onions. Pour in clam juice and 2 tablespoons of the lemon juice. Bring to a boil over high heat; then cover, reduce heat, and simmer until fish flakes readily when prodded in thickest portion with a fork (3 to 5 minutes). Lift out and keep warm.

Boil cooking liquid over high heat until reduced to ¾ cup; set aside. In a small pan, melt remaining 2 tablespoons butter over medium heat; stir in flour and cook until bubbly. Gradually whisk in reduced cooking liquid, milk, remaining 1 tablespoon lemon juice, mustard, and nutmeg; cook, stirring, until bubbly and thickened.

Arrange 2 cups of the sorrel on a rimmed platter; top with sole. Stir remaining 1 cup sorrel into sauce; then spoon about half the sauce over sole and garnish with remaining onions and lemon wedges. Pour remaining sauce into a bowl; pass to spoon on individual servings. Makes 4 servings.

Chayote Crab Casserole

Chayote (chi-*yo*-de), the fruit of a tropical vine native to Central America, is finding its way into more and more North American markets. Its flesh tastes like delicate summer squash; the soft edible seed has a nutlike flavor.

    3 medium-size chayotes (about 2 lbs.
        total), cut into 1-inch cubes
    8 tablespoons (¼ lb.) butter or margarine
    1 cup sliced mushrooms
    1 small onion, chopped
    ⅓ cup all-purpose flour
 1¾ cups milk
    ¼ cup dry sherry
    1 can (6½ oz.) crabmeat, drained
        Salt and white pepper
 1½ cups soft bread crumbs

Boil chayotes as directed on page 17 until almost tender when pierced (about 12 minutes); drain well.

Melt 2 tablespoons of the butter in a wide frying pan over medium-high heat. Add mushrooms and onion; cook until mushrooms are lightly browned and liquid has evaporated. Add 4 tablespoons of the remaining butter; stir in flour and cook until bubbly. Gradually stir in milk and sherry and cook, stirring, until sauce boils and thickens. Stir in crab and chayote; season to taste with salt and pepper. Pour into a shallow 2-quart casserole.

Melt remaining 2 tablespoons butter in a small pan over medium heat; stir in bread crumbs, then sprinkle evenly over crab mixture. Bake, uncovered, in a 350° oven for about 30 minutes or until hot throughout. Makes 6 servings.

Eggplant Parmesan Casserole

For a vegetarian version of this dish, just omit the beef from the sauce.

    1 large eggplant (about 1½ lbs.)
    1 pound lean ground beef
    1 medium-size onion, chopped
    ¼ pound mushrooms, sliced
    1 clove garlic, minced or pressed
    1 large can (15 oz.) tomato sauce
    ¾ teaspoon *each* dry basil and oregano
        leaves
        Salt and pepper
 1½ cups (6 oz.) shredded mozzarella cheese
    ½ cup grated Parmesan cheese

Bake eggplant as directed on page 24. Meanwhile, crumble beef into a wide frying pan over medium heat; cook, stirring, until browned. Add onion,

mushrooms, and garlic; cook, stirring, until onion is soft. Add tomato sauce, basil, and oregano; simmer, uncovered, for 10 minutes. Season to taste with salt and pepper.

Evenly arrange about half the eggplant in a shallow 2-quart casserole; top with half the sauce, then half the mozzarella cheese and half the Parmesan cheese. Repeat layers.

Bake, uncovered, in a 350° oven for about 25 minutes or until hot and bubbly. Makes 6 servings.

Almond Turkey with Peas

Two kinds of peas—shelled and edible-pod—transform leftover turkey into a special meal.

- ¼ **cup slivered almonds**
- 2 **tablespoons butter or margarine**
- ½ **pound mushrooms, sliced**
- 1½ **cups shelled green peas (about 1½ lbs. unshelled) or 1 package (10 oz.) frozen peas**
- ½ **pound edible-pod peas, ends and strings removed, or 1 package (6 oz.) frozen edible-pod peas**
- ¾ **cup regular-strength chicken broth**
- ½ **cup sliced canned water chestnuts**
- 2 **to 3 cups bite-size pieces cold cooked turkey or chicken**
- ⅓ **cup sliced green onions (including tops)**
- 4 **teaspoons cornstarch**
- 1 **tablespoon soy sauce**
  Hot cooked rice

Spread almonds in a shallow pan and toast in a 350° oven for about 8 minutes or until lightly browned; set aside.

Melt butter in a wide frying pan over medium heat. Add mushrooms and cook, stirring, until lightly browned. Add shelled and edible-pod peas and ½ cup of the broth. Bring to a boil; then cover, reduce heat, and simmer, stirring often, until fresh peas are tender to bite or frozen peas are thawed (about 5 minutes). Add water chestnuts, turkey, and onions; cook, stirring, for 1 more minute.

In a small bowl, combine cornstarch, soy, and remaining ¼ cup broth; stir into turkey mixture and cook, stirring, until bubbly and thickened.

Spoon each serving over hot cooked rice; garnish with almonds. Makes 4 to 6 servings.

Simple boiled or steamed vegetables get a flavor boost from lively seasoned butters. You can store any of these butters in the refrigerator for several weeks; for longer storage, freeze them by shaping the prepared butter into a log and wrapping it in foil. You can simply cut off slices of the frozen log to melt over piping hot vegetables.

Each of the following recipes makes about ½ cup—enough to season 8 servings.

Dill Butter. In a bowl, mix ½ cup (¼ lb.) softened **butter** or margarine, 1 teaspoon **lemon juice** and teaspoon **dill weed** until well blended.

Garlic Butter. In a bowl, mix ½ cup (¼ lb.) softened **butter** or margarine, 2 or 3 cloves **garlic** (minced or pressed), and 2 tablespoons minced **parsley** until well blended.

Fresh Herb Butter. In a blender or food processor, combine ½ cup (¼ lb.) softened **butter** or margarine, ½ cup lightly packed leaves of **fresh basil**, chives, mint, parsley, or watercress, and 1 teaspoon **lemon juice.** Whirl until smooth.

Herb-Cheese Butter. In a bowl, combine ½ cup (¼ lb.) softened **butter** or margarine, 1 tablespoon minced **parsley**, ½ teaspoon **Italian herb seasoning**, ¼ teaspoon **garlic salt**, ⅛ teaspoon **pepper**, and 3 tablespoons grated **Parmesan cheese.** Mix until well blended.

Lemon Butter. In a bowl, mix ½ cup (¼ lb.) softened **butter** or margarine, ¾ teaspoon grated **lemon peel**, 4 teaspoons **lemon juice**, and ¼ cup minced **parsley** until well blended.

Spiced Butter. In a bowl, combine ½ cup (¼ lb.) softened **butter** or margarine, 3 tablespoons firmly packed **brown sugar**, ¼ teaspoon *each* ground **cinnamon** and **allspice**, and ⅛ teaspoon ground **nutmeg.** Mix until well blended.

Vegetable & Egg Burritos

Eggs, cheese, and whatever fresh vegetables you have on hand make a tasty filling for warm tortillas. When you need a meal in a hurry, try this simple, satisfying entrée.

    8 to 10 flour tortillas
    8 eggs
    2 tablespoons water
    ¼ teaspoon *each* garlic salt and pepper
    3 tablespoons butter or margarine
    2 large carrots or zucchini, chopped
    3 green onions (including tops), thinly
       sliced
    1 can (4 oz.) diced green chiles
    1 cup corn cut from cob (about 1 large ear)
       or 1 can (about 9 oz.) whole kernel corn,
       drained
    1 cup (4 oz.) shredded Cheddar or jack
       cheese
    1 can (2¼ oz.) sliced ripe olives, drained,
       or 1 tomato or avocado
       Butter, romaine, or iceberg lettuce
       leaves
       Prepared taco sauce
       Sour cream (optional)

Wrap tortillas in foil; heat in a 350° oven for 15 to 20 minutes or until warm.

Meanwhile, beat together eggs, water, garlic salt, and pepper until blended. Melt 2 tablespoons of the butter in a wide frying pan with an oven-proof handle over medium-low heat. Add carrots and cook, stirring often, until tender (3 to 5 minutes). Stir in onions, chiles, and corn; cook, stirring often, until hot. Melt remaining 1 tablespoon butter in pan; pour in egg mixture. When eggs begin to set, push cooked portion aside to allow un-cooked eggs to flow underneath.

When eggs are almost set, remove tortillas from oven. Broil egg mixture in pan about 4 inches below heat just until set on top. Sprinkle with cheese and broil just until cheese is melted.

Remove pan from broiler and garnish with olives. (Or dice tomato; or peel, pit, and dice avocado. Then sprinkle either tomato or avocado over egg mixture.)

Line each tortilla with a lettuce leaf; spoon egg mixture down center. Top with taco sauce and, if desired, a dollop of sour cream; roll up. Makes 4 servings.

Harvest Chicken with Roasted Vegetables

Pictured on facing page

Maximize your oven's energy—and save your own—with this one-pan oven dinner: herb-fragrant roast chicken surrounded by colorful fresh vegetables.

    4 to 6 thin-skinned potatoes, *each* 2 to 3
       inches in diameter
    1 broiler-fryer chicken (3½ to 4 lbs.)
    3 large carrots, cut into 1½-inch chunks
    4 small pattypan squash
    3 medium-size crookneck squash, cut into
       1½-inch chunks
    2 large red or green bell peppers,
       quartered and seeded
    2 cloves garlic, quartered
    1 large onion, quartered
    6 to 8 cherry tomatoes
   10 to 12 sprigs fresh rosemary or 1 teaspoon
       dry rosemary

Pierce potatoes in several places and set on rack in oven as it preheats to 375°. Remove chicken giblets and reserve for other uses. Rinse chicken, pat dry, and place, breast side up, in a 12 by 15-inch pan (not on a rack).

Arrange carrots, pattypan squash (leave whole), crookneck squash, peppers, garlic, onion, and tomatoes around chicken. Cut 2 or 3 of the rosemary sprigs into 2 to 3-inch pieces; place on vegetables. (Or sprinkle vegetables with dry rosemary.)

Roast, uncovered, in oven with potatoes for 1 to 1¼ hours or until meat near thighbone is no longer pink when slashed and potatoes feel soft when squeezed. Stir vegetables occasionally while chicken is roasting.

Transfer chicken to a large platter; carefully lift vegetables from pan with a slotted spoon and mound alongside chicken.

Attractively arrange remaining rosemary sprigs around chicken or tuck them into chicken cavity. Spoon pan juices over vegetables; serve potatoes separately. Makes 4 to 6 servings.

LATE SUMMER'S BOUNTY of bright garden produce glows in this colorful presentation of Harvest Chicken with Roasted Vegetables (recipe on this page).

Spaghetti Squash Supper

For an unusual entrée, mound seasoned ribbons of baked spaghetti squash in the shell halves; then top with stir-fried broccoli and sausage.

> 1 **spaghetti squash (3½ to 4 lbs.)**
> **Soy-Ginger Sauce (recipe follows)**
> 2 **tablespoons salad oil**
> 1½ **to 2 cups bite-size pieces broccoli flowerets and peeled stalks**
> 1 **pound kielbasa (Polish sausage), thinly sliced**
> 4 **tablespoons butter or margarine, softened**
> **Garlic salt and pepper**

Bake squash as directed on page 24. Prepare Soy-Ginger Sauce; set aside.

Heat oil in a wok or wide frying pan over high heat; add broccoli and cook, stirring constantly, until tender-crisp to bite (3 to 4 minutes). Lift out and set aside. Add sausage and cook, stirring, until browned. Discard drippings; return broccoli to pan along with Soy-Ginger Sauce and keep warm over low heat.

Cut squash in half lengthwise; scrape out and discard seeds. Loosen squash strands; mound in shell halves. Stir in butter and season to taste with garlic salt and pepper. Top with broccoli mixture; pass pan juices at the table. Makes 6 servings.

Soy-Ginger Sauce. Mix ½ cup **soy sauce**, 2 tablespoons **apple juice**, 2 teaspoons *each* **brown sugar** and sliced **green onion** (including top), and ½ teaspoon **ground ginger.**

Zucchini Lasagne

Thin slices of zucchini stand in for pasta in this rendition of an Italian favorite. A generous helping of meat sauce and cheese makes it hearty enough to satisfy the hungriest diners.

> **Meat Sauce (recipe follows)**
> 6 **medium-size zucchini, cut lengthwise into ⅛-inch slices**
> 8 **ounces mozzarella cheese, thinly sliced**
> 1 **cup (8 oz.) ricotta cheese**
> ½ **cup grated Parmesan cheese**

Prepare Meat Sauce and set aside.

Arrange half the zucchini in a greased 9 by 13-inch baking dish. Top evenly with half the mozzarella cheese, half the ricotta cheese, and half the sauce. Repeat layers. Sprinkle Parmesan cheese evenly over all. (At this point, you may cover and refrigerate until next day.)

Bake, uncovered, in a 350° oven for 35 minutes (45 to 55 minutes if refrigerated) or until zucchini is tender when pierced. Makes 6 to 8 servings.

Meat Sauce. Heat 2 tablespoons **salad oil** in a wide frying pan over medium heat; add 1 large **onion** (chopped) and 2 cloves **garlic** (minced or pressed). Cook, stirring, until onion is soft; then add ¼ pound **mushrooms** (sliced) and ½ pound **lean ground beef.** Cook, stirring, for 5 minutes. Stir in 1 can (about 1 lb.) **tomatoes** (break up with a spoon) and their liquid, 1 can (6 oz.) **tomato paste,** ¾ cup **dry red wine** or regular-strength beef broth, 1½ teaspoons **oregano leaves,** and ½ teaspoon **dry basil.** Season to taste with **salt** and **pepper.** Boil gently, stirring often, until thick (about 25 minutes).

Curried Okra

Okra is probably best known for its starring role in Creole gumbo, but it's also used in West Indian cooking.

> 2 **tablespoons salad oil**
> 1 **medium-size onion, chopped**
> 4 **to 6 teaspoons curry powder**
> 1 **pound lean ground beef**
> 1 **large can (28 oz.) tomatoes**
> 1½ **pounds okra or 2 packages (10 oz. *each*) frozen okra**
> **Salt and pepper**
> **Hot cooked rice**
> **Condiments (suggestions follow)**

Heat oil in a wide frying pan over medium heat; add onion and cook, stirring, until soft. Stir in curry powder and cook for 2 to 3 more minutes. Crumble in beef and cook, stirring, until browned; then add tomatoes (break up with a spoon) and their liquid.

Trim and discard stem ends from fresh okra, then stir into beef mixture (or separate frozen okra). Bring to a boil over high heat; then cover, reduce heat, and simmer until okra is tender to bite

(about 30 minutes for fresh okra, 20 minutes for frozen). Season to taste with salt and pepper.

Spoon okra mixture over hot cooked rice; pass 3 or more condiments to sprinkle on individual servings. Makes 4 servings.

Condiments. In separate bowls, place **plain yogurt**, shredded **coconut, raisins, salted peanuts,** and chopped **Major Grey's chutney.**

Beef & Vegetable Soup

Warm up skiers and snowman-makers on a chilly winter evening with a big pot of hearty soup.

- ¼ pound sliced bacon, cut into 1-inch pieces
- ¾ pound lean ground beef
- 1 medium-size onion, chopped
- 1 large stalk celery, chopped
- 1 medium-size green pepper, seeded and chopped
- 1 large can (28 oz.) tomatoes
- 2 large carrots, cut into ½-inch-thick slices
- 2 large thin-skinned potatoes, cut into ½-inch cubes
- 5 cups water
- 1 bay leaf
- 2 cloves garlic, minced or pressed
- 3 to 4 teaspoons chili powder
- 3 beef bouillon cubes
- 1 package (10 oz.) frozen lima beans, thawed
- ½ small head green cabbage, coarsely shredded
   Salt and pepper
   Grated Parmesan cheese

In an 8 to 10-quart kettle over medium-high heat, cook bacon for 5 minutes. Crumble beef into kettle and cook, stirring, until lightly browned. Add onion, celery, and green pepper and cook, stirring, until onion is soft. Add tomatoes (break up with a spoon) and their liquid, carrots, potatoes, water, bay leaf, garlic, chili powder, and bouillon cubes; mix well. Bring to a boil over high heat; then cover, reduce heat, and simmer for 1 hour.

Stir in beans and cabbage. Bring to a boil over high heat; then cover, reduce heat, and simmer until cabbage is tender to bite (15 to 20 minutes).

Skim off fat; season to taste with salt and pepper. If made ahead, cool, cover, and refrigerate until next day. To reheat, place kettle over medium-high heat until soup is boiling. Pass cheese to sprinkle on individual servings. Makes about 20 cups.

Tomato Beef Stew

This stew is a little different from the traditional dish: vegetables are just briefly steamed—to maintain crisp texture and lively, distinct flavors—and added to the stew during the last minutes of cooking.

- 1 pound top round steak
- 2 tablespoons salad oil
- 1 large onion, chopped
- 1 large green or red bell pepper, seeded and chopped
- ½ pound mushrooms, sliced
- 1 large can (28 oz.) tomatoes
- 1 can (8 oz.) tomato sauce
- 1 teaspoon paprika
- ¼ teaspoon *each* thyme leaves, marjoram leaves, and pepper
- ¼ cup dry red wine
- 2 large turnips, peeled and cut into ¾-inch chunks
- 6 small carrots, sliced
- 3 large stalks celery, sliced

Trim and discard excess fat from meat; cut meat into 1-inch cubes. Heat oil in a 5 to 6-quart kettle over medium heat; add meat, a portion at a time, and cook until browned on all sides. Lift out and set aside. Add onion and green pepper to kettle and cook, stirring, until onion is soft. Stir in mushrooms and cook until liquid has evaporated (2 to 3 more minutes).

Return meat to kettle; add tomatoes (break up with a spoon) and their liquid, tomato sauce, paprika, thyme, marjoram, pepper, and wine. Bring to a boil over high heat; then cover, reduce heat, and simmer until meat is tender when pierced (about 1½ hours).

Meanwhile, arrange turnips and about half the carrots on a steaming rack. Steam as directed for carrots on page 17, cooking only until vegetables are barely tender to bite (5 to 8 minutes). Lift out and set aside. Repeat with remaining carrots and celery. Add vegetables to meat mixture during last 10 minutes of cooking. Makes 4 servings.

Pumpkin Patch Lamb Stew

Pictured on facing page

Celebrate Hallowe'en with this "trick or treat" special. The trick: a whole pumpkin becomes an edible baking and serving dish. The treat's inside the pumpkin—a spicy, savory lamb stew.

> 1 **pumpkin, about 10 inches in diameter**
> **About 2 tablespoons salad oil**
> 2½ **pounds lean boneless lamb, cut into**
>   **1-inch cubes**
> 2 **large onions, chopped**
> 2 **cloves garlic, minced or pressed**
> 1 **whole cinnamon stick (about 2 inches)**
> ⅛ **teaspoon *each* ground cloves and ginger**
>   **Dash of ground red pepper (cayenne)**
> 2 **cups regular-strength chicken broth**
> 5 **medium-size carrots**
> 2 **large zucchini, cut into ½-inch slices**
> 2 **tablespoons *each* all-purpose flour and**
>   **water**
>   **Cinnamon sticks (optional)**

Cut a lid about 6 inches in diameter from top of pumpkin. Scrape out seeds, fibers, and some of the flesh, leaving a ¾ to 1-inch-thick shell. Wrap stem with foil, replace lid, and place pumpkin in a shallow roasting pan. Add water to a depth of ½ inch; bake, uncovered, in a 350° oven for about 1 hour or until almost tender when pierced.

Heat 1 tablespoon of the oil in a 5-quart kettle over medium-high heat; add meat, a portion at a time, and cook until lightly browned. Remove meat from kettle and set aside. Add remaining 1 tablespoon oil to kettle if necessary; then add onions and garlic. Cook, stirring, until onions are soft; return meat and juices to kettle. Add cinnamon stick, cloves, ginger, red pepper, and broth. Bring to a boil over high heat; then cover, reduce heat, and simmer until meat is tender when pierced (about 1 hour).

Cut carrots in half lengthwise, then cut halves into 1-inch pieces. Add carrots and zucchini to meat; cover and simmer for 5 minutes. With a slotted spoon, transfer meat and vegetables to hot pumpkin; discard cinnamon stick. Mix flour and water until smooth and stir into kettle juices.

Cook, stirring, until mixture boils and thickens. Pour into pumpkin. Set lid in place and bake in pan for 30 minutes or until pumpkin is tender when pierced. Remove foil from stem.

Using several wide spatulas, carefully transfer pumpkin to a serving platter. At the table, spoon stew onto individual plates, scooping out some of pumpkin's inside flesh as you serve. Garnish with cinnamon sticks, if desired. Makes 4 to 6 servings.

Red Pepper Chowder

Bits of bright red bell pepper add sweet flavor and sparks of color to this creamy white fish chowder.

> 4 **tablespoons butter, margarine, or**
>   **salad oil**
> 2 **medium-size onions, chopped**
> ½ **pound mushrooms, sliced**
> 1 **tablespoon lemon juice**
> 2 **large red bell peppers, seeded and cut**
>   **into thin strips**
> 2 **cans (14½ oz. *each*) regular-strength**
>   **chicken broth**
> 1 **pound thin-skinned potatoes, sliced**
> 2 **tablespoons *each* cornstarch and water**
> ½ **pint (1 cup) sour cream**
> 1½ **to 2 pounds boneless, skinless white**
>   **fish (such as halibut, rockfish, red**
>   **snapper, or sole)**
> ½ **cup minced parsley**
>   **Salt and pepper**
>   **Lemon wedges**

Melt butter in a 4 to 5-quart kettle over medium-high heat. Add onions, mushrooms, lemon juice, and peppers; cook, stirring, until vegetables are soft (about 5 minutes). Add broth and potatoes. Bring to a boil over high heat; then cover, reduce heat, and simmer until potatoes are tender when pierced (about 15 minutes).

In a small bowl, mix cornstarch and water until smooth; stir in sour cream. Gradually stir in some of the soup liquid, then, stirring gently, pour back into kettle and bring to a boil over high heat.

Cut fish into bite-size chunks; add fish and parsley to soup. Return to boil; then cover, reduce heat, and simmer until fish flakes readily when prodded with a fork (about 5 minutes). If made ahead, cool, cover, and refrigerate until next day; reheat until steaming. Season to taste with salt and pepper. Pass lemon wedges. Makes 14 cups.

GREAT PUMPKIN reigns over autumn feast featuring colorful **Pumpkin Patch Lamb Stew** (recipe on this page). Spicy entrée is baked in the pumpkin, then served over rice.

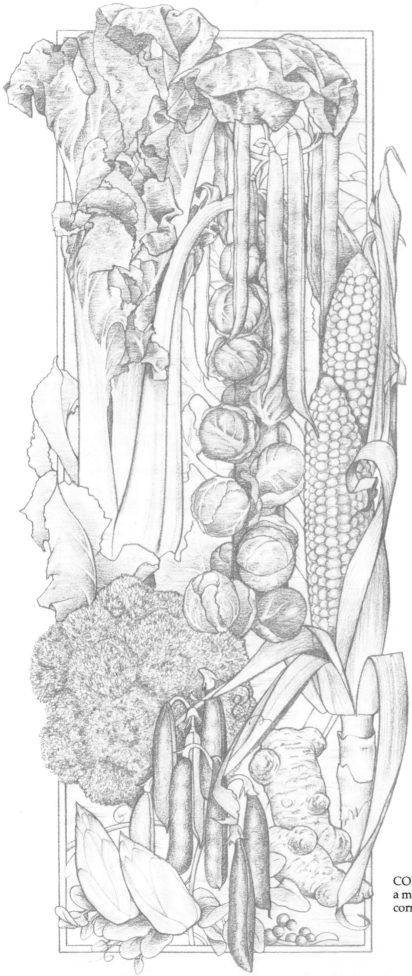

Side Dishes

*T*hese recipes will persuade you that the right side dish can make the difference between an ordinary meal and a memorable one, and that any entrée will taste better with a well-chosen vegetable dish adding contrasting flavor, color, and texture.

The recipes we offer here can put an end to ho-hum dining —any one of them will pep up a family meal or add a little class to a party dinner. Take your choice from carefully seasoned solo vegetables or combinations; avoid the rush with our make-ahead dishes; or simply glamorize steamed carrots or broccoli with an enticing sauce.

COMELY COMPANIONS add color, flavor, and variety to a menu: bok choy, green beans, a stalk of Brussels sprouts, corn, broccoli, green peas, sunchokes, Belgian endive.

Sautéed Greens

Balance a spicy or richly sauced entrée with a fresh-tasting, colorful side dish of greens. Or pair these greens with roast pork, ham, or sausages.

　　About 1½ pounds collard greens or kale
　3 or 4 strips bacon
　1 clove garlic, minced or pressed
　½ cup regular-strength chicken broth
　　Salt and pepper

Rinse and prepare collard greens as directed on page 9; cut into strips and set aside.

In a 4 to 5-quart kettle over medium heat, cook bacon until crisp; then remove from pan, drain, crumble, and set aside. Discard all but 2 tablespoons drippings. Add garlic, greens, and broth to pan and cook, stirring, for 2 minutes; then cover and continue to cook, stirring often, until greens are tender to bite (about 15 more minutes).

Drain, if necessary; then season to taste with salt and pepper and transfer to a serving dish. Top with bacon. Makes about 4 servings.

Simmered Artichoke Hearts

Reaching the tender heart of a thorny artichoke is just a matter of following a few simple steps. After simmering in herb-seasoned broth, succulent hearts are ready to serve—either unembellished or dressed up with a sauce or filling.

　6 artichokes, *each* at least 3 inches in
　　diameter
　2 cups regular-strength chicken broth
　½ cup dry vermouth
　¼ cup olive oil or salad oil
　2 cloves garlic
　1 teaspoon thyme leaves
　1 bay leaf
　⅛ teaspoon dry basil
　⅛ teaspoon summer savory or oregano
　　leaves

Trim stem of artichoke flush with bottom. Pull off and discard small, tough base bracts (leaves). Snap back large bracts; then pull each one away, leaving meaty base attached to artichoke bottom; reserve

leaves for other uses, if desired. Continue removing bracts down to pale, very thin inner leaves. Slice these leaves flush with top of base and discard; then cut away remaining fibrous portions on base to make heart look smooth and neat. Immediately plunge heart into acidulated water (3 tablespoons lemon juice or vinegar per quart water) while you prepare remaining artichokes.

In a 4 to 5-quart kettle, combine broth, vermouth, oil, garlic, thyme, bay leaf, basil, and savory; add hearts. Bring to a boil over high heat; then cover, reduce heat, and simmer until tender when pierced (about 30 minutes). Drain, reserving broth. When hearts are cool enough to handle, scoop out and discard fuzzy centers (chokes).

Serve hot. If made ahead, cool in broth; then cover and refrigerate until next day. Serve cold, or reheat hearts in broth over medium heat. Makes 6 servings.

Asparagus Spears with Egg Dressing

Fresh asparagus spears topped with tangy egg dressing can lead a double life: served hot, they're a delicious accompaniment to springtime's roast lamb or chicken; chilled, they're a perfect starter for warm-weather meals.

　4 hard-cooked eggs, chopped
　¼ cup *each* chopped celery and parsley
　¼ cup mayonnaise
　1 tablespoon *each* lemon juice and grated
　　Parmesan cheese
　1 teaspoon Dijon mustard
　¼ teaspoon *each* celery salt and dill weed
　2 bunches asparagus (about 2 lbs. *total*)

In a bowl, combine eggs, celery, parsley, mayonnaise, lemon juice, cheese, mustard, celery salt, and dill. If made ahead, cover and refrigerate until next day.

Snap off and discard tough ends of asparagus; peel stalks, if desired. Boil as directed on page 16 until tender when pierced (7 to 10 minutes). Drain well. (At this point, you may rinse in cold water, drain, cover, and refrigerate until next day.)

Arrange hot or cold spears side by side on a platter; spoon egg dressing across centers of spears. Makes about 6 servings.

Savory Beans & Tomatoes

Pictured on facing page

Thin, tender green or wax beans, fresh from market or garden, go fancy in this make-ahead dish—sure to become a dinner party favorite. Steamed beans are combined with ripe tomatoes and aromatic herbs, then baked with a buttery, garlicky topping of crumbs and cheese.

2½ pounds green or wax beans, cut into
  2-inch pieces
4 large tomatoes
10 tablespoons (¼ lb. plus 2 tablespoons)
  butter or margarine
1 large onion, chopped
½ pound mushrooms, sliced
3 cloves garlic, minced or pressed
1 teaspoon *each* dry basil, oregano
  leaves, and salt
1½ cups soft bread crumbs
⅓ cup grated Parmesan cheese
½ teaspoon *each* dry basil and oregano
  leaves

Arrange beans on a steaming rack; steam as directed on page 16 until tender when pierced (8 to 12 minutes). Rinse in cold water and drain. Cut tomatoes into thin wedges; set aside.

Melt 4 tablespoons of the butter in a wide frying pan over medium-high heat. Add onion, mushrooms, and ⅔ of the garlic. Cook, stirring, until onion is soft and all liquid has evaporated. Stir in the 1 teaspoon basil, oregano, and salt. Combine mushroom mixture with beans and tomatoes; transfer to a shallow 3-quart baking dish.

Melt remaining 6 tablespoons butter in a small pan. Stir in remaining garlic, crumbs, cheese, and the ½ teaspoon basil and oregano. (At this point, you may cover and refrigerate beans and topping separately for up to 2 days.)

Sprinkle crumb mixture over beans. Cover and bake in a 400° oven for 20 minutes (30 minutes if refrigerated); uncover and bake for 5 more minutes or until hot throughout. Makes 12 to 15 servings.

Garden Patch Sauté

Melted cream cheese with pimentos provides a smooth, rich coating for these stir-fried vegetables.

½ cup slivered almonds
2 small onions
1 pound green beans
¼ pound mushrooms
2 ears corn
3 to 4 tablespoons salad oil
1 can (2¼ oz.) sliced ripe olives, drained
1 package (3 oz.) cream cheese with
  pimentos, cut into chunks
  Mexican seasoning, lemon pepper
  seasoning, and salt

Spread almonds in a shallow baking pan and toast in a 350° oven for about 8 minutes or until golden; set aside.

Cut onions into thin lengthwise slices and cut beans diagonally into ½ to ¾-inch slices. Slice mushrooms lengthwise; cut corn kernels off cobs. Keep vegetables separate.

Heat 2 tablespoons of the oil in a wok or wide frying pan over high heat; add onions and beans and cook, stirring, for 3 minutes. Add remaining 1 to 2 tablespoons oil, mushrooms, and corn; cook, stirring, for 2 minutes. Add olives and cream cheese; season to taste with Mexican seasoning, lemon pepper seasoning, and salt. Stir until cheese is melted. Pour into a warm serving dish and top with almonds. Makes 4 to 6 servings.

Mustard-glazed Carrots

Even avowed carrot haters will ask for a second helping of sweet, tender-crisp sliced carrots cloaked with a tangy mustard glaze.

2 pounds carrots, cut diagonally into
  ¼-inch-thick slices
3 tablespoons *each* Dijon mustard and
  butter or margarine
2 tablespoons firmly packed brown sugar
  Chopped parsley

Boil carrots as directed on page 17 until tender-crisp to bite (5 to 10 minutes). Drain well. Stir in mustard, butter, and sugar; cook, stirring, over medium heat until carrots are glazed (1 to 2 minutes). Sprinkle with parsley. Makes 6 servings.

AROMATIC HERBS, garlic, and a topping of seasoned bread crumbs enhance Savory Beans & Tomatoes (recipe on this page), a dish bold enough to complement robust meats.

Three-way Mixed Vegetables

Cooking dinner for a houseful of guests is a big undertaking, so it's helpful to plan dishes that can be prepared ahead. You can assemble these vegetables early in the day or on the night before, then finish preparing them—in one of three ways—just before dinner.

> 1 **pound carrots**
> 1½ **pounds broccoli**
> 1 **medium-size head cauliflower**

Cut carrots into ¼-inch-thick diagonal slices. Cut broccoli flowerets off stalks; slice large ones in half lengthwise. Trim and discard base of stalks; then peel stalks and cut into ¼-inch-thick slices. Separate cauliflower into flowerets; cut large ones in half lengthwise through stems.

Arrange carrots, broccoli stems, and cauliflowerets on a steaming rack; steam as directed for carrots on page 17 until vegetables are just tender when pierced (about 9 minutes). Add broccoli flowerets; steam until just tender when pierced (about 1½ more minutes). Plunge vegetables into cold water to cool them quickly; drain. (At this point, you may cover and refrigerate until next day.) Use in any of the following recipes. Makes 10 to 12 servings.

Creamy Mixed Vegetables. Melt 5 tablespoons **butter** or margarine in a 3-quart pan over medium heat. Add 5 tablespoons **all-purpose flour** and cook, stirring, until bubbly. Gradually stir in 2¾ cups **milk.** Cook, stirring, until sauce boils and thickens. Stir in 1 tablespoon **Dijon mustard,** ½ teaspoon **pepper,** 1½ cups (6 oz.) shredded **Swiss cheese,** and 2 tablespoons chopped **parsley.** Season to taste with **salt.** Cook, stirring, until cheese is melted.

Pour half the sauce into a shallow 3-quart casserole. Add cooked vegetables; mix gently, then top with remaining sauce and mix again. Sprinkle with ¼ cup toasted **sesame seeds.** Bake in a 375° oven for about 30 minutes (40 to 45 minutes if vegetables were refrigerated) or until hot throughout.

Marinated Mixed Vegetables. Stir together ½ cup **salad oil,** ¼ cup **white wine vinegar,** 1 clove **garlic** (minced or pressed), ½ teaspoon **salt,** and ⅛ teaspoon **pepper.** Place carrots and cauliflower in a large bowl. Pour marinade over vegetables, mix gently, cover, and refrigerate for at least 4 hours or until next day. Just before serving, gently stir in broccoli stems and flowerets. Serve cold or at room temperature.

Mixed Vegetables in Pesto Butter. Melt 3 tablespoons **butter** or margarine in a wide frying pan over medium heat. Add 1 carton (4 oz.) **frozen pesto sauce,** thawed. Add cooked vegetables, stirring gently. Cover and cook, stirring often, until hot throughout (7 to 10 minutes).

Green Bean & Zucchini Bundles

Individual portions of green beans are dressed with a faintly sweet basil-honey vinaigrette. Serve the bundles as a salad or a vegetable side dish; the eye-catching presentation makes them ideal for a buffet.

> 1 **large zucchini, at least 2 inches in diameter**
> 1½ **pounds green beans, ends trimmed**
> ½ **cup salad oil**
> ¼ **cup white wine vinegar**
> 2 **tablespoons** *each* **Dijon mustard and honey**
> 2 **small cloves garlic, minced or pressed**
> 2 **tablespoons chopped fresh basil or 2 teaspoons dry basil**

Cut off and discard ends from zucchini, then cut squash crosswise into 8 equal slices. With a small knife, cut out centers of zucchini slices, leaving a ¼-inch rim. Reserve centers for other uses, if desired.

Arrange beans on a steaming rack. Steam as directed on page 16, cooking only until just tender-crisp to bite (about 10 minutes). Plunge immediately into cold water; when cool, drain.

Arrange zucchini rings on a steaming rack. Steam as directed on page 18, cooking only until just tender when pierced (2 to 3 minutes). Plunge immediately into cold water; when cool, drain.

Poke 8 to 10 beans through each zucchini ring. Arrange bundles in a shallow dish. (At this point, you may cover and refrigerate until next day.) In a small bowl, combine oil, vinegar, mustard, honey, garlic, and basil; pour over bean bundles. Makes 8 servings.

Purists may insist on vegetables adorned only with a pat of butter—but we think it's worthwhile to take an occasional trip into the realm of the *saucier*. Our versatile béchamel is a dressed-up white sauce rich with broth and cream. With the addition of cheese, it becomes mornay sauce; a little spice transforms it into a curry sauce. Egg and butter-enriched hollandaise or béarnaise cloaks simply prepared vegetables in grand style.

Béchamel Sauce

    2 tablespoons butter or margarine
    2 tablespoons all-purpose flour
    ½ cup regular-strength chicken or beef broth
    ½ cup half-and-half (light cream)
      Salt and freshly grated or ground nutmeg

Melt butter in a small pan over medium heat. Add flour and cook, stirring, until bubbly. Gradually pour in broth and half-and-half; cook, stirring, until sauce boils and thickens. Season to taste with salt and nutmeg. Use hot. Or let cool; then cover and refrigerate until next day. To serve, reheat over medium heat, stirring constantly. Makes about 1 cup.

Mornay Sauce. Prepare **Béchamel Sauce,** but when sauce comes to a boil, reduce heat and stir in 2 tablespoons shredded **Gruyère** or Swiss cheese and 2 tablespoons grated **Parmesan cheese.** Remove from heat and season to taste with **salt** and **ground red pepper (cayenne);** omit nutmeg. Thin with additional cream, if desired. Makes about 1 cup.

Curry Sauce. Prepare **Béchamel Sauce,** but stir 2 teaspoons **curry powder** and ⅛ teaspoon **ground ginger** into melted butter along with flour. Season to taste with **salt** and **pepper;** omit nutmeg. Makes about 1 cup.

Hollandaise

An all-yolk hollandaise sauce will be thicker, more golden, and richer-tasting than a sauce made with whole eggs.

    1 egg or 3 egg yolks
    1 teaspoon Dijon or other prepared
      mustard
    1 tablespoon lemon juice or white wine
      vinegar
    1 cup (½ lb.) butter or margarine, melted
      and hot

In a blender or food processor, whirl egg, mustard, and lemon juice until well blended. With motor on high, add butter, a few drops at a time at first, increasing to a slow, steady stream about ¹⁄₁₆ inch wide as mixture begins to thicken. Serve immediately; or if sauce is to be used within several hours, let stand at room temperature.

To reheat, place container of sauce in water that's just warm to touch; stir constantly with a whisk for about 1 minute. Transfer to water that's hot to touch; stir until sauce is warm.

If made further ahead, cover and refrigerate for up to 1 week; bring to room temperature before reheating. Makes 1 to 1½ cups.

Béarnaise

    1 tablespoon minced shallot or onion
    ½ teaspoon dry tarragon
    2 tablespoons white wine vinegar
      Hollandaise (recipe above)

In a small pan over medium heat, combine shallot, tarragon, and vinegar. Cook, stirring, until liquid has evaporated. Prepare Hollandaise as directed, adding shallot mixture (hot or cold) to egg, mustard, and lemon juice. Makes 1 to 1½ cups.

Broccoli with Bacon

Quick and simple to prepare, this broccoli dish pairs well with fish and cheese entrées. The easy bacon and crumb topping perks up cooked cauliflower or spinach, too.

> 1 **pound broccoli**
> 4 **strips bacon**
> ¼ **cup minced green onions (including tops)**
> ¾ **cup fine dry bread crumbs**

Cut off and discard base of broccoli stalks; peel stalks, if desired. Cut lengthwise into spears; slash through bottom inch of stalks. Boil spears as directed on page 16 until just tender when pierced (7 to 10 minutes).

In a wide frying pan over medium heat, cook bacon until crisp; drain, crumble, and set aside. In drippings, cook onions until wilted; stir in crumbs and mix well. Drain broccoli; arrange on a hot platter and sprinkle with bacon and crumbs. Makes 3 or 4 servings.

Spinach-stuffed Tomatoes

Pictured on facing page

Summer's finest vine-ripened tomatoes, filled with a savory mixture of spinach and Parmesan, make a perfect warm-weather complement to cold meats.

> 8 **medium-size tomatoes**
> 1 **tablespoon butter or margarine**
> 1 **tablespoon salad oil**
> 1 **medium-size onion, chopped**
> ¾ **pound spinach, coarsely chopped**
> 1¼ **cups (about 4 oz.) shredded Parmesan cheese**
> 2 **tablespoons fine dry bread crumbs**
> ⅛ **teaspoon ground nutmeg**

Cut off the top fourth of each tomato; reserve for other uses, if desired. With a small spoon, scoop out pulp to make hollow shells. Chop pulp and place in a colander to drain.

Melt butter with oil in a wide frying pan over medium-high heat. Add onion and cook, stirring, until onion is soft. Stir in reserved tomato pulp and spinach and cook, stirring, until spinach is wilted (3 to 4 minutes). Stir in 1 cup of the cheese, crumbs, and nutmeg.

Fill each tomato with spinach mixture and arrange in an ungreased baking pan; sprinkle evenly with remaining ¼ cup cheese. Broil 4 inches below heat until cheese is lightly browned (3 to 4 minutes). Makes 8 servings.

Potatoes Anna

Pictured on facing page

In France, the humble *pomme de terre* (literally, "apple of the earth") often gets star treatment. Here's one example: a buttery potato cake encased in thin, crisp golden potato slices.

> **About 3 pounds russet potatoes**
> 1 **cup (½ lb.) butter or margarine, melted**
> **Salt (optional)**

Peel potatoes, dropping each into cold water to prevent browning. With a thin-bladed sharp knife, cut potatoes into paper-thin (about ¹⁄₁₆-inch) slices, returning slices to cold water as you cut them.

Pour about 4 tablespoons of the butter into a 2-inch-deep 9 or 10-inch frying pan with an ovenproof handle. Tilt pan to coat bottom and sides.

Drain potato slices, spread on a towel, and pat dry. Carefully arrange a layer of potatoes in pan in an overlapping pattern. Drizzle with about 2 tablespoons of the butter. Repeat layers of potatoes and butter until all potatoes are used (sprinkle each layer with salt, if desired). Pour any remaining butter over top and around sides of pan.

Place pan over medium heat and cook until potatoes begin to brown around pan sides (15 to 20 minutes); then bake, uncovered, in a 450° oven for 40 minutes or until potatoes are very tender when pierced. Baste occasionally with butter in pan. Let cool for 10 minutes; then hold potatoes in place with a wide spatula and drain excess butter from pan (reserve for other uses, if desired). Run a knife around pan edge, then invert potatoes onto serving plate. If any potatoes stick to pan, carefully pry free and fit onto potato cake. Cut into wedges. Makes 6 to 8 servings.

CRUSTY BROWN and buttery Potatoes Anna (recipe on this page) share the spotlight with Spinach-stuffed Tomatoes (recipe on this page) and succulent roast beef.

Savory Brussels Sprouts

Briefly steamed until barely tender, then warmed gently in a simple sauce, Brussels sprouts are a sprightly addition to dinner. Spoon sour cream over the sprouts at the table.

    About 1 pound Brussels sprouts
  3 strips bacon
  1 tablespoon butter or margarine
  1 medium-size onion, chopped
  2 small tomatoes, seeded and diced
    Salt and freshly ground pepper
    Sour cream

Trim sprouts, cut in half lengthwise, and rinse. Arrange on a steaming rack; steam as directed for whole Brussels sprouts on page 16 until just tender when pierced (8 to 10 minutes). Drain well.

Meanwhile, in a wide frying pan over medium heat, cook bacon until crisp; remove from pan, drain, crumble, and set aside.

Discard all but 2 tablespoons drippings. Add butter and onion to pan and cook, stirring, until onion is soft. Stir in tomatoes and bacon; cook until hot throughout. Stir in hot sprouts; season to taste with salt and pepper. Pour into a serving dish. Pass sour cream to spoon over individual servings. Makes 4 servings.

Chard & Cabbage Stir-fry

Our Chinese-inspired stir-fry of tangy cabbage and succulent Swiss chard can double as a salad. Since it goes together quickly, you'll want to have all the ingredients ready before you start to cook.

  1 small head green cabbage (about 1¼ lbs.)
  1 bunch Swiss chard (about 1¼ lbs.)
  2 tablespoons sesame seeds
  3 strips bacon
  1 large onion, thinly sliced
  1 clove garlic, minced or pressed
  1 tablespoon *each* soy sauce and water

Shred cabbage as directed on page 14; you should have about 5 cups. Cut chard leaves from stalks. Thinly slice stalks, then coarsely chop leaves; keep separate.

In a wok or wide frying pan over medium heat, toast sesame seeds, stirring constantly, until golden; remove from wok. Add bacon and cook until crisp. Remove from pan; drain, crumble, and set aside. Pour off and reserve all but 1 tablespoon drippings.

Add onion to drippings in wok; raise heat to high and cook, stirring constantly, for 2 minutes. Add cabbage and chard stalks; cook for 4 minutes, stirring constantly, adding more drippings if needed. In a small bowl, combine garlic, soy, and water. Stir into cabbage mixture along with chard leaves; cook until leaves are wilted (about 2 more minutes).

Pour into a serving dish; sprinkle with bacon and sesame seeds. Makes 6 servings.

Nutty Eggplant Casserole

Eggplant slices bake beneath layers of garden vegetables, buttery bread crumbs, and grated cheese in this flavorful casserole. Chopped peanuts add a tasty crunch.

  2 eggplants (*each* about 1 lb.)
  4 strips bacon, diced
  1 small onion, chopped
  1 small green or red bell pepper, seeded and chopped
  3 medium-size tomatoes, peeled and chopped
  1 cup chopped salted peanuts
  ½ cup grated Parmesan cheese
  1 tablespoon butter or margarine
  ½ cup soft bread crumbs
  ½ teaspoon paprika

Bake eggplants as directed on page 24 until well browned and tender when pierced (20 to 30 minutes).

Meanwhile, in a wide frying pan over medium heat, cook bacon until crisp; remove from pan, drain, and set aside. Discard all but 2 tablespoons drippings; add onion and green pepper and cook, stirring, until onion is soft. Stir in tomatoes; set aside.

Place eggplant slices in a shallow 2-quart casserole. Top evenly with onion mixture, then sprinkle evenly with bacon, peanuts, and cheese. Melt butter in a small pan; stir in crumbs. Distribute

crumbs and paprika evenly over top of casserole. Bake, uncovered, in a 350° oven for 20 minutes or until hot throughout. Makes 6 to 8 servings.

Fennel with Red Bell Pepper

Fresh fennel resembles celery in appearance—but the taste is entirely different. The creamy white bulb and feathery green leaves have a mild licorice flavor that pairs perfectly with seafood. Next time you serve fish for dinner, add to the menu this simple, elegant dish of fennel in cream.

    3 or 4 fennel bulbs with tops
    2 tablespoons butter or margarine
    1 small onion, chopped
    1 small red bell pepper, seeded and
       chopped
    ½ cup whipping cream

Cut off fennel leaves; chop enough to make ¼ cup and set aside. Cut off and discard stalks. Cut bulbs in half lengthwise; then cut crosswise into ¼-inch-thick slices.

   Melt 1 tablespoon of the butter in a wide frying pan over medium heat. Add onion and bell pepper and cook, stirring occasionally, until onion is soft. Add remaining 1 tablespoon butter and fennel slices to the pan. Cook, stirring, until fennel is just tender-crisp to bite (about 2 minutes). Transfer to a serving dish.

   Pour cream into pan. Bring to a boil over high heat and continue to boil, stirring, until reduced by half. Pour over fennel mixture and sprinkle with fennel leaves. Makes 4 to 6 servings.

Sweet Baked Parsnips

The parsnip, a pale yellow cousin of the carrot, bakes to a mellow sweetness when sliced and glazed with brown sugar.

    6 medium-size parsnips (about 1 lb.
       total), peeled
    ¼ cup firmly packed brown sugar
    2 ounces lean salt pork, finely diced
    1 cup water

Cut parsnips into pieces about 2½ inches long; then cut each piece lengthwise into ¼-inch-thick slices. Place in a 9-inch square baking dish. Sprinkle sugar evenly over parsnips, then top evenly with salt pork. Pour in water. Bake, uncovered, in a 350° oven for about 1 hour or until parsnips are tender when pierced and pork is browned; stir parsnips several times while baking. Makes 4 to 6 servings.

Peas & Onions in Cream Sauce

For many people, a traditional holiday menu just isn't complete without this time-honored accompaniment for meats or poultry. You can cook the vegetables and sauce a day ahead, ready to combine and reheat before serving.

    About 3 dozen small white boiling
       onions
    2 quarts water
    6 cups shelled peas (6 to 7 lbs.
       unshelled) or 4 packages (10 oz. *each*)
       frozen peas, thawed
    2 tablespoons butter or margarine
    1½ tablespoons all-purpose flour
    ½ teaspoon *each* sugar, white pepper,
       ground nutmeg, and salt
    1 pint (2 cups) half-and-half (light
       cream)

Peel onions as directed on page 11.

   In a 4 to 5-quart kettle, bring water to a boil over high heat. Add onions; then reduce heat and simmer, uncovered, for 12 minutes. Add shelled peas; continue to cook, uncovered, until vegetables are barely tender when pierced (about 5 more minutes). Pour into a colander, rinse under cold running water, and drain.

   Melt butter in kettle over medium heat; stir in flour, sugar, pepper, nutmeg, and salt. Cook, stirring, until bubbly. Gradually add half-and-half, stirring constantly. Cook, stirring, until sauce boils and thickens. (At this point, you may cover and refrigerate vegetables and sauce separately until next day.)

   In kettle, combine cooked or thawed peas, onions, and cream sauce. Cook over medium heat, stirring frequently, just until hot throughout (10 to 15 minutes). Makes 14 to 16 servings.

Mellowed Rutabaga

A golden purée of rutabaga, carrots, and yam is studded with crunchy diced jicama. This sweet combination of roots and tubers is a painless way to introduce the oft-slandered rutabaga to skeptical tasters.

> 1 large rutabaga (about ¾ lb.)
> 3 large carrots
> 1 large yam (about ¾ lb.)
> ⅔ cup peeled and finely diced jicama or drained and diced water chestnuts
> 4 tablespoons butter or margarine, softened
> ⅛ teaspoon ground nutmeg
> Salt and pepper
> ⅓ cup slivered almonds

Cut rutabaga, carrots, and yam into 1-inch cubes. In a 3 to 4-quart pan, bring 2 to 3 inches water to a boil over high heat. Add vegetables, cover, and cook until very tender when pierced (about 25 minutes); drain. Mash vegetables with a potato masher or beat with an electric mixer until smooth; you should have 3 to 3½ cups. Stir in jicama, butter, and nutmeg; season to taste with salt and pepper. Spoon into a 1 to 1½-quart shallow casserole. Sprinkle evenly with almonds. Bake, uncovered, in a 375° oven for 20 minutes or until hot throughout. Makes about 6 servings.

Baked Squash with Maple Butter

Squash halves baked with maple syrup and spicy butter make a sweet accompaniment for pork or ham.

> 3 large acorn squash
> ½ cup (¼ lb.) butter or margarine
> 6 tablespoons maple syrup or honey
> ½ teaspoon ground cinnamon
> ¼ teaspoon *each* ground ginger and allspice

Prepare and bake squash as directed on page 25. (At this point, you may cool, cover, and refrigerate for up to 3 days.)

In a bowl, beat together butter, syrup, cinnamon, ginger, and allspice. If made ahead, cover and refrigerate for up to 3 days.

Place squash, cut side up, in a large shallow baking dish; place about a sixth of the maple butter in each cavity. Cover and bake in a 400° oven for 10 minutes (25 minutes if refrigerated) or until hot throughout. For each serving, scoop out flesh and some of the maple butter with a spoon. Makes about 12 servings.

Potatoes in a Pastry Shell

If Crisp Potato Skins (page 28) become a favorite appetizer, use the reserved flesh to prepare this elegant dish. No one will ever guess you started with leftovers!

> 5 large baked russet potatoes (page 24)
> ⅓ cup butter or margarine, melted
> ¼ cup whipping cream, heated
> ½ cup finely chopped parsley
> 3 cloves garlic, minced or pressed
> 1 teaspoon Italian herbs
> Salt and pepper
> 4 frozen patty shells, thawed
> 1 egg

Scoop out flesh from baked potatoes; you should have about 4 cups. In a large bowl, combine potatoes, butter, cream, parsley, garlic, and herbs. Blend gently with a fork (do not mash). Season to taste with salt and pepper.

Stack 2 patty shells; roll out on a lightly floured board to a 9½-inch round. Transfer to a 10 by 15-inch baking sheet. Stack remaining shells; roll out to a 10½-inch round.

Mound potato mixture in center of smaller round, leaving a ½-inch pastry border. Top with larger round. Fold bottom edge over top, pressing firmly with fork or fingers to seal tightly. Pat top to flatten.

Beat egg lightly; brush over pastry. Slash pastry top in 3 places. Bake on lowest rack of a 400° oven for 25 minutes or until golden brown. With a wide spatula, transfer to a platter; cut into wedges. Makes 6 to 8 servings.

WHEN THE BARBECUE BECKONS, serve Crunchy Potato Salad (recipe on page 49), brimming with raw vegetables, along with grilled Polish sausage, rye bread, and beer.

"Putting Up" the Harvest Bounty for Year-round Enjoyment

Mother Nature's gifts arrive in fits and starts. For months, we can't find the fresh vegetables we long for—vine-ripened tomatoes, sweet red peppers, tender summer squash. Then suddenly, gardeners and grocers alike are reeling from bumper crops.

You don't have to resign yourself to this "feast or famine" schedule, though. When your favorite vegetables are in season—or on special at the market—preserve or freeze them in relishes, sauces, and other specialties.

Fresh Tomato Sauce

- 3 tablespoons salad oil
- 2 large onions, finely chopped
- 4 cloves garlic, minced or pressed
- 5 pounds tomatoes (about 12 medium-size), peeled, cored, and cut into eighths
- 1 large green pepper, seeded and chopped
- 1 teaspoon salt
- ¾ teaspoon *each* pepper and dry rosemary
- ¼ teaspoon anise seeds, crushed
- 1 tablespoon *each* dry basil, oregano leaves, and sugar
- 1 teaspoon paprika
- ¾ cup dry red wine

Heat oil in a 6-quart kettle over medium heat; add onions and garlic and cook, stirring often, until onion is soft (about 10 minutes). Stir in tomatoes, green pepper, salt, pepper, rosemary, anise seeds, basil, oregano, sugar, paprika, and wine. Bring to a boil over high heat, stirring to break up tomatoes. Cover, reduce heat, and simmer for 1 hour.

Uncover and boil over medium-high heat, stirring often, until mixture is reduced to 8 cups (about 50 minutes).

Use hot. Or let cool, then cover and refrigerate for up to 3 days; or freeze for up to 4 months. To reheat, thaw if frozen, then bring to simmering over low heat, stirring occasionally. Makes 8 cups.

Summer Squash Relish

- 20 medium-size zucchini or crookneck squash (about 5 lbs. *total*)
- 2 large onions
- 4 medium-size carrots
- 2 large red bell peppers, seeded
- 5 tablespoons salt
- 3 cups sugar
- 2½ cups white (distilled) vinegar
- 1 tablespoon *each* ground nutmeg and turmeric
- 2 teaspoons celery seeds
- 1 teaspoon *each* dry mustard and pepper

With a food chopper or food processor, finely chop zucchini, onions, carrots, and peppers. Combine vegetables in a 6-quart kettle, add water to cover, and stir in salt. Cover and refrigerate for at least 4 hours or until next day.

Drain vegetables, rinse well, and drain again. Return to kettle along with sugar, vinegar, nutmeg, turmeric, celery seeds, mustard, and pepper. Bring to a boil over high heat. Reduce heat to medium and cook, uncovered, stirring often, until thick (about 40 minutes). Fill 7 hot, sterilized pint-size canning jars to within ½ inch of rims. Wipe rims clean; top with scalded lids, then screw on bands. Process in a boiling water bath for 15 minutes. Let cool; test for a seal. Makes 7 pints.

Duxelles

- 4 tablespoons butter or margarine
- 1 small onion, finely chopped
- 1 pound mushrooms, finely chopped
- 1 clove garlic, minced or pressed
  Salt, pepper, and ground nutmeg

Melt butter in a wide frying pan over medium-high heat; add onion and cook, stirring, until soft. Add mushrooms and garlic and cook, stirring, until liquid has evaporated (about 15 minutes). Season to taste with salt, pepper, and nutmeg. Let cool; then cover and refrigerate for up to 1½ weeks. Or freeze small amounts on a baking sheet lined with wax paper; when solid, store in plastic bags (thaw before using). Makes about 2 cups.

Duxelles and Chive Dip. In a small bowl, mix ⅓ cup **sour cream,** 2 tablespoons **duxelles,** and 1 teaspoon finely chopped **chives** or green onion (including top). Season to taste with **salt, pepper,** and **ground nutmeg.** Serve as a dip for raw vegetables; or spoon over lightly cooked green beans or zucchini. Makes about ½ cup.

Duxelles and Parmesan Sauce. In a small bowl, mix ¼ cup grated **Parmesan cheese** and 2 tablespoons *each* **duxelles** and **mayonnaise.** Spoon over 3 or 4 servings of baked chicken or fish fillets about halfway through baking time. Makes about ½ cup.

Duxelles Appetizers. Prepare **Duxelles and Parmesan Sauce** and spoon about ½ teaspoon on **melba toast rounds.** Place on an ungreased baking sheet and broil about 4 inches below heat just until cheese sizzles (2 to 3 minutes).

Spicy Red Pepper Jam

>   8 cups seeded and chopped red bell peppers (about 10 medium-size)
>   1 tablespoon salt
>   3 cups sugar
>   1 bottle (12.8 oz.) white wine vinegar
>   ¼ teaspoon ground nutmeg

Place peppers in a large bowl. Add water to cover, then stir in salt. Let stand at room temperature for 2 hours. Drain, rinse well, and drain again.

In a 5-quart kettle, combine peppers, sugar, vinegar, and nutmeg; bring to a boil over high heat. Reduce heat to medium and cook, uncovered, stirring often, until mixture is thick (about 40 minutes).

Ladle hot jam into hot, sterilized ½-pint canning jars to within ⅛ inch of rims. Wipe rims clean; top with scalded lids, then screw on bands. Let cool; test for a seal. Makes 5 half-pints.

Pickle-packed Vegetables

>   1 medium-size mild white onion, thinly sliced
>   4 cups prepared vegetables (directions follow)
>   1 cup white (distilled) vinegar
>   ⅔ cup sugar
>   1 clove garlic, minced or pressed (optional)

In a clean wide-mouth quart jar, firmly pack onion and your choice of vegetable (or a combination such as carrots and cauliflower) in alternate layers.

In a 2-cup glass measure, combine vinegar, sugar, and, if desired, garlic. Stir until sugar is dissolved; pour over vegetables to fill jar. Screw on lid and shake jar well; refrigerate at least until next day or for as long as 3 months. Makes 1 quart.

Cucumbers and zucchini. Cut 2 or 3 medium-size cucumbers or zucchini into ¼-inch slices. Place in a bowl, sprinkle with 1 tablespoon salt, add water to cover, and let stand for 1 to 2 hours; drain.

Beets. Boil 6 to 8 medium-size beets as directed on page 16. Peel and cut into ¼-inch slices.

Carrots, turnips, and cauliflower. Peel 5 or 6 medium-size carrots or turnips and cut into ¼-inch slices; or separate 1 medium-size head cauliflower into flowerets (cut large ones in half lengthwise). Arrange on a steaming rack and steam as directed on pages 17 and 18.

Mashed Potatoes

Try our traditional mashed potatoes when you're planning a special meal for a crowd.

    4 to 5 pounds russet potatoes
    ⅔ cup (¼ lb. plus about 3 tablespoons) butter or margarine, softened
    ⅔ to ¾ cup milk
    Salt and pepper

Peel potatoes and cut into quarters; drop cut pieces into cold water to prevent browning.

In a 5-quart kettle, heat 1 inch of water to boiling over high heat. Add potatoes; then cover, reduce heat, and simmer until potatoes are tender when pierced (about 20 minutes). Drain well.

Mash hot potatoes with a potato masher or beat with an electric mixer until no lumps remain. Add butter; beat until well blended. Stir in milk, a little at a time, until potatoes reach desired consistency. Season to taste with salt and pepper. Makes 14 to 16 servings.

Ratatouille

Pictured on facing page

This classic vegetable stew from France's Mediterranean region is popular in the United States, as well. Ratatouille is a perfect make-ahead dish—it tastes even better a few days after it's made, and it's wonderful whether it's served hot or at room temperature.

    ¼ cup olive oil or salad oil
    2 large onions, sliced
    2 large cloves garlic, minced or pressed
    1 medium-size eggplant, cut into ½-inch cubes
    6 medium-size zucchini, thickly sliced
    2 green or red bell peppers, seeded and cut into strips
    2 teaspoons dry basil
    ½ cup minced parsley
    5 large tomatoes, cut into wedges
    Salt

Heat oil in a wide frying pan over medium-high heat. Add onions and garlic and cook, stirring, until onions are soft. Stir in eggplant, zucchini, peppers, basil, and parsley. Reduce heat to medium; then cook, uncovered, stirring occasionally, for 30 minutes.

Add 4 of the tomatoes and stir to blend. Cook, uncovered, stirring occasionally, until eggplant is very tender when pierced (about 15 minutes). Season to taste with salt.

Serve hot or at room temperature, garnished with the remaining tomato. If made ahead, cool, cover, and refrigerate for up to 1 week. Makes 8 to 10 servings.

Layered Yam Casserole

A crunchy honey-nut topping decorates this casserole for a crowd. You can prepare it ahead, then pop it into the oven an hour before dinner. It's a good choice to accompany baked ham or turkey.

    3½ to 4 pounds yams
    ¼ cup sliced almonds
    1 large onion, thinly sliced
    3 oranges
    ½ cup (¼ lb.) butter or margarine, melted
    2 tablespoons honey
    Salt and pepper

Boil yams as directed on page 17 until tender when pierced (20 to 30 minutes). Let cool; then peel and cut diagonally into ¼-inch-thick slices.

Spread almonds in a shallow pan and toast in a 350° oven for about 8 minutes or until golden; set aside. Arrange a third of the yams in an even layer in a shallow 3-quart baking dish. Top with half the onion; then arrange another third of the yams atop onion. Top with remaining onion and yams.

Remove and discard peel and white membrane from 2 of the oranges; then slice oranges and arrange on top of yams. Squeeze juice from remaining orange and combine with butter and honey; pour evenly over yam mixture. Sprinkle lightly with salt and pepper. (At this point, you may cover and refrigerate until next day.)

Sprinkle almonds over top of casserole and bake, covered, in a 325° oven for 45 to 50 minutes (about 1 hour if refrigerated) or until hot throughout. Makes 8 to 10 servings.

PROVENÇAL PARADE—ripe summer vegetables combine in popular Ratatouille (recipe on this page), an aromatic vegetable stew from the sunny south of France.

Breads & Desserts

*T*here's just no end to vegetables' versatility. Here
they show up in breads—
yeast and quick, and in an array
to enhance the entire day, from
breakfast, through afternoon
coffee or tea, through dinner.
And then they appear in
desserts—cake, pie, tarts, and a
unique apple crisp.

Wherever they're used, they
enrich, contributing nutrition,
flavor, and moistness and making any occasion more special.

UNEXPECTED CONTRIBUTIONS to the goodness
of breads, pies, and cakes: chayote, tomatoes,
pumpkin, carrots, sweet potatoes, and summer
squash (zucchini varieties, crookneck, pattypan).

Mushroom Bread

Savory mushroom-flecked batter is baked in a coffee can with a wide foil collar; the result is a fancifully shaped loaf that looks—and tastes—like a mushroom.

       2 **tablespoons butter or margarine**
      ¼ **pound mushrooms, minced**
      ¾ **cup milk**
       2 **tablespoons sugar**
       1 **teaspoon** *each* **minced parsley and instant minced onion**
      ¼ **teaspoon thyme leaves**
    1½ **teaspoons garlic salt**
       1 **package active dry yeast**
      ⅓ **cup warm water (about 110°)**
       1 **egg**
    2¾ **to 3 cups all-purpose flour**

Melt butter in a small frying pan over medium heat. Add mushrooms and cook, stirring, until liquid has evaporated. Add milk, sugar, parsley, onion, thyme, and garlic salt; heat until warm (about 110°).

In a large bowl, dissolve yeast in water. Add mushroom mixture; beat in egg and 1½ cups of the flour. Gradually beat in 1¼ to 1½ cups more flour to make a heavy, stiff batter that is too sticky to knead. Cover and let rise in a warm place (80°) until almost doubled (45 minutes to 1 hour).

Meanwhile, generously grease a 1-pound coffee can. Fold an 18 by 22-inch piece of heavy-duty foil in half crosswise to make an 18 by 11-inch rectangle. Crumple in edges of foil to form a circle 8 inches in diameter; crimp edges up to make a rim. Grease foil; then center circle over can opening. With scissors, punch a hole in center of foil; then make several evenly spaced cuts from center to edges of can, forming triangular flaps. Remove foil and grease between the 2 layers of the flaps so they stick together; also grease reverse sides of flaps. Replace foil on top of can and press flaps down around inside of can.

When dough has risen, stir it down; then spoon dough into prepared can. Top of dough should come slightly above flap tips, holding them in place against inside of can. Place can upright on a shallow baking sheet. Let dough rise in a warm place (80°), uncovered, until mushroom cap measures about 7½ inches across and is about 2½ inches above top of can (30 to 45 minutes).

Bake on lowest rack of a 350° oven for about 50 minutes or until well browned. Place, cap side down, on a wire rack; at once, gently lift off can. Let cool slightly, then carefully peel off foil collar. Serve warm or cooled.

To slice, cut off mushroom loaf's stem just below the cap; then slice stem and cap into individual pieces. Makes 1 loaf.

Garden Quick Loaves

Pictured on page 94

When your garden swamps you with tomatoes or zucchini, try this tasty bread. Moist, sweet slices are great for snacking or with a soup or salad.

       2 **cups prepared tomatoes or zucchini (directions follow)**
       3 **cups all-purpose flour**
       1 **teaspoon** *each* **salt and baking soda**
      ½ **teaspoon baking powder**
       2 **teaspoons ground cinnamon**
       1 **cup chopped nuts**
       3 **eggs**
    1½ **cups sugar**
       1 **cup salad oil**
       1 **teaspoon vanilla**

To prepare tomatoes, peel 3 or 4 medium-size tomatoes. Cut each in half and squeeze gently to remove seeds. Chop pulp finely; you should have 2 cups. Set aside.

To prepare zucchini, coarsely shred about 2 medium-size zucchini and pack lightly into a measuring cup; you should have 2 cups. Set aside.

In a bowl, stir together flour, salt, baking soda, baking powder, cinnamon, and nuts; set aside.

In another bowl, lightly beat eggs with a wire whisk. Add sugar and oil; stir until blended. Stir in vanilla and vegetable. Add flour mixture all at once and stir just until dry ingredients are moistened. Spoon batter evenly into 2 greased and flour-dusted 4½ by 8½-inch loaf pans.

Bake in a 350° oven for 50 minutes to 1 hour or until a wooden pick inserted in centers comes out clean. Let cool in pans on wire racks for 10 minutes; then turn out onto racks to cool completely. Before slicing, wrap tightly and refrigerate until next day or for up to 1 week; or freeze for longer storage. Makes 2 loaves.

Potato Cinnamon Buns

Pictured on facing page

Bake plump, buttery cinnamon buns from a traditional European potato yeast dough.

    1 pound russet potatoes
    2 cups milk
    1 cup (½ lb.) butter or margarine
    1 cup plus 2 tablespoons sugar
    1 teaspoon salt
    2 packages active dry yeast
    ½ cup warm water (about 110°)
    8 to 8½ cups all-purpose flour
    2 eggs
    2 teaspoons vanilla
       Cinnamon Filling (recipe follows)
       Nut Glaze (recipe follows)

Pour water into a 3 to 4-quart pan to a depth of 1 inch; bring to a boil over high heat. Add potatoes and cook, covered, until tender when pierced (30 to 40 minutes). Drain; then peel and mash with a potato masher or beat with an electric mixer until smooth. You should have 2 cups. Place potatoes in a pan over medium heat and slowly stir in milk until smooth. Add ½ cup of the butter, 1 cup of the sugar, and salt; heat until warm (about 110°).

In a large bowl, combine yeast, water, and remaining 2 tablespoons sugar; let stand until bubbly (5 to 15 minutes). Add potato mixture, 4 cups of the flour, eggs, and vanilla; beat until smooth and well blended. Gradually stir in 3½ to 4 cups more flour, about 1 cup at a time, to make a stiff dough.

Turn dough out onto a heavily floured board and knead until smooth and elastic (about 15 minutes), adding more flour as necessary to prevent sticking. Place dough in a greased bowl, then turn over to grease top. Cover and let rise in a warm place (80°) until almost doubled (about 1½ hours).

Meanwhile, prepare Cinnamon Filling.

Punch dough down and knead briefly to release air; divide dough in half.

Melt remaining ½ cup butter in a small pan. Roll out one portion of dough at a time on a floured board to a 15 by 18-inch rectangle. Brush with 3 tablespoons of the melted butter and sprinkle with half the Cinnamon Filling. Starting at the long side, roll up dough jelly roll style; then cut crosswise into 12 equal slices. Place slices, cut side down, in a greased 9 by 13-inch baking pan; brush

with 1 more tablespoon of the melted butter. Cover and let rise in a warm place (80°) until almost doubled (35 to 45 minutes).

Bake in a 350° oven for 30 minutes or until browned. Meanwhile, prepare Nut Glaze.

Let buns cool slightly. Remove from pans and place on wire racks; drizzle with Nut Glaze, and serve warm. Or let cool completely, then wrap and freeze. To reheat, unwrap and let thaw; then cover lightly and place in a 350° oven for 20 minutes or until hot throughout. Drizzle with Nut Glaze. Makes 2 dozen buns.

Cinnamon Filling. In a bowl, mix 2 tablespoons **ground cinnamon,** ¾ cup *each* **granulated sugar** and firmly packed **brown sugar,** and 1 cup **raisins.**

Nut Glaze. In a bowl, stir together 3 cups unsifted **powdered sugar,** ½ cup chopped **nuts,** ¼ teaspoon **ground cinnamon,** 2 tablespoons **butter** or margarine (melted), and 4 to 5 tablespoons **water.**

Leaf Lettuce Bread

Leaf lettuce isn't just for salads—here, it makes a surprise appearance in a tasty quick bread.

    1½ cups all-purpose flour
     2 teaspoons baking powder
     ½ teaspoon *each* baking soda and salt
     ⅛ teaspoon *each* ground ginger and mace
     ½ cup salad oil
     1 cup sugar
     2 eggs
    1½ teaspoons grated lemon peel
     1 cup lightly packed, finely chopped
        green or red leaf lettuce
     ½ cup chopped nuts

In a small bowl, stir together flour, baking powder, baking soda, salt, ginger, and mace. In another bowl, combine oil, sugar, eggs, and lemon peel. Add flour mixture, stirring until smooth; then stir in lettuce and nuts. Pour into a greased and flour-dusted 4½ by 8½-inch loaf pan.

Bake in a 350° oven for 50 to 55 minutes or until a wooden pick inserted in center comes out clean. Let cool in pan on a wire rack for 10 minutes; then turn out onto rack to cool completely. Makes 1 loaf.

LURE LATE RISERS from their slumbers with Potato Cinnamon Buns (recipe on this page). Add fresh fruit of the season and coffee for a pleasing continental breakfast.

Spicy Pineapple Zucchini Bread

Pictured on page 94

Tangy pineapple and moist zucchini make a winning flavor combination in this easy, tender quick bread. Spread slices lavishly with cream cheese and serve as an accompaniment to fruit salad or afternoon tea.

  3 eggs
  1 cup salad oil
  2 cups sugar
  2 teaspoons vanilla
  2 cups coarsely shredded unpeeled zucchini
  1 can (8¼ oz.) crushed pineapple, drained well
  3 cups all-purpose flour
  2 teaspoons baking soda
  1 teaspoon salt
  ½ teaspoon baking powder
  1½ teaspoons ground cinnamon
  ¾ teaspoon ground nutmeg
  1 cup *each* currants and finely chopped walnuts

In a large bowl, beat eggs until frothy. Add oil, sugar, and vanilla; continue beating until mixture is thick and foamy. Stir in zucchini and pineapple. In another bowl, combine flour, baking soda, salt, baking powder, cinnamon, nutmeg, currants, and walnuts; stir until thoroughly blended. Stir flour mixture into zucchini mixture just until dry ingredients are moistened. Spoon batter evenly into 2 greased and flour-dusted 9 by 5-inch loaf pans.

Bake in a 350° oven for 1 hour or until a wooden pick inserted in centers comes out clean. Let cool in pans on wire racks for 10 minutes; then turn out onto racks to cool completely. Before slicing, wrap tightly and refrigerate until next day. Makes 2 loaves.

Jicama Apple Crisp

You've probably served jicama strips as appetizers, and tossed crisp, sweet pieces into salads or stir-fry dishes. But have you ever served it for dessert? If not, start here—include jicama slices in a crumb-topped apple crisp for extra sweetness and crunch.

  2 medium-size Golden Delicious apples
  1¼ to 1½ pounds jicama
  ⅓ cup apple juice
  ¼ cup granulated sugar
  ¼ teaspoon ground nutmeg
  ½ cup firmly packed brown sugar
  1 teaspoon ground cinnamon
  ¼ teaspoon salt
  ¾ cup all-purpose flour
  4 tablespoons butter or margarine

Peel, core, and quarter apples. Cut quarters into ¾-inch-thick slices; you should have about 2 cups. Peel jicama and cut into pieces about ⅛ inch thick and ¾ inch square; you should have about 4 cups.

Combine apples and jicama and spoon into a greased 9-inch square baking dish. Stir together apple juice, granulated sugar, and nutmeg; pour over apple mixture. In a bowl, combine brown sugar, cinnamon, salt, and flour. With a pastry blender or two knives, cut in butter until particles are about the size of small peas. Squeeze small handfuls of the mixture together, then crumble evenly over apple mixture in coarse chunks.

Bake in a 375° oven for about 35 minutes or until topping is browned and apples are tender when pierced. Makes 6 to 8 servings.

Walnut Carrot Cake

Pictured on page 94

Shredded carrot makes this spicy butter cake especially sweet and moist.

  1 cup (½ lb.) butter or margarine, softened
  2 cups firmly packed dark brown sugar
  4 eggs
  1 teaspoon vanilla
  ¼ cup buttermilk
  2 cups lightly packed shredded carrots
  ¾ cup chopped walnuts
  2½ cups all-purpose flour
  1½ teaspoons baking soda
  2 teaspoons ground cinnamon
  ½ teaspoon *each* ground nutmeg, ground cloves, and ground allspice
  ¼ teaspoon salt
    Cream Cheese Frosting (recipe follows)
    Preserved kumquats or walnut halves

In a large bowl, cream butter and sugar until light and fluffy. Add eggs, one at a time, beating well after each addition; then beat in vanilla and buttermilk. Stir in carrots and walnuts.

In another bowl, combine flour, baking soda, cinnamon, nutmeg, cloves, allspice, and salt; then stir into carrot mixture.

Spread batter in a greased, flour-dusted 9 by 13-inch baking pan. Bake in a 350° oven for about 40 minutes or until a wooden pick inserted in center comes out clean. Let cool in pan on a wire rack for 25 minutes; then invert onto rack and let cool completely. Spread top with Cream Cheese Frosting. Cut into squares and decorate each with a kumquat. Makes 12 servings.

Cream Cheese Frosting. In a small bowl, combine 1 package (3 oz.) **cream cheese** (softened), 3 tablespoons **butter** or margarine (softened), and 1 teaspoon **vanilla.** Beat until smooth; then gradually beat in 2 cups **powdered sugar** until smooth.

Crookneck Pie

Pictured on page 94

Looking for an unusual dessert? Try this one: a bright yellow pie with an intriguing texture.

- 4 **small crookneck squash (about 1 lb. *total*)**
- ¾ cup **flaked coconut**
- 3 tablespoons **all-purpose flour**
- 1⅓ cups **sugar**
- ¾ teaspoon **ground nutmeg**
- ¼ teaspoon **salt**
- ¼ cup *each* **lemon juice and orange juice**
  Sesame Seed Crust (recipe follows)
- 5 **eggs**
- 1 cup **toasted flaked coconut (optional)**

Cut squash in half lengthwise. Scoop out and discard seeds, then finely shred squash; you should have 2½ cups. In a bowl, combine squash, the ¾ cup coconut, flour, sugar, ½ teaspoon of the nutmeg, salt, lemon juice, and orange juice. Stir well.

Prepare Sesame Seed Crust. Beat eggs lightly; add to squash mixture and stir well. Pour into crust and sprinkle remaining ¼ teaspoon nutmeg on top. Bake in a 350° oven for 55 minutes or until a knife inserted in center comes out clean. Let cool in pan on a wire rack. If desired, garnish with the 1 cup toasted coconut. Makes 6 servings.

Sesame Seed Crust. In a bowl, combine 1¼ cups **all-purpose flour,** ¼ cup **sesame seeds,** and ¼ teaspoon **salt.** With a pastry blender or two knives, cut ½ cup **solid shortening** into flour mixture until it resembles coarse crumbs. Gradually stir in 3½ tablespoons **ice water.** Roll dough out on a floured board and fit into a 9-inch pie pan; flute edges.

Pumpkin Tartlets

Pictured on page 94

Perfect party dessert: spicy, creamy pumpkin tarts. One taste and we think you'll agree that pumpkin pie is not only for Thanksgiving.

- **Pastry for a double-crust 9-inch pie**
- 2 **eggs**
- ⅔ cup **firmly packed dark brown sugar**
- 2 cups **Pumpkin Purée (directions follow) or 1 can (1 lb.) pumpkin**
- 1½ teaspoons **ground cinnamon**
- ½ teaspoon **salt**
- ½ teaspoon *each* **ground cloves, nutmeg, allspice, and ginger**
- 1½ cups **half-and-half (light cream)**
  Sweetened Whipped Cream (optional)

Shape pastry into a roll and cut into 16 equal portions (about 4 teaspoons *each*). Press each portion evenly over bottom and up sides of a 3-inch brioche tin. Place tins on a baking sheet; set aside.

In a large bowl, beat eggs and sugar until creamy. Add pumpkin, cinnamon, salt, cloves, nutmeg, allspice, and ginger. Stir until well blended. Gradually pour in half-and-half; beating until mixture is smooth. Pour about ¼ cup of the filling into each pastry shell. Bake in a 400° oven for about 30 minutes or until a knife inserted in centers comes out clean. Let cool in tins on wire racks until cool enough to handle; then carefully tip tartlets out of tins and place on a serving tray. Garnish with whipped cream, if desired. Makes 16 tartlets.

Pumpkin Purée. Bake a 10-pound **pumpkin** as directed on page 25 until flesh is tender when pierced. Let pumpkin cool until you can handle it; then scoop out flesh. In a blender or food processor, whirl flesh, a portion at a time, until smooth. Pour purée into a wire strainer and let drain until as thick as mashed potatoes (about 30 minutes). If made ahead, cover and refrigerate for up to 2 days; or freeze for longer storage. Makes 5 to 8 cups.

Index

SILVER SHIMMERS beneath these treats: (from left) Crookneck Pie (page 93), Pumpkin Tartlets (page 93), Garden Quick Loaves (page 89), Walnut Carrot Cake (page 92), and Spicy Pineapple Zucchini Bread (page 92).

Metric Conversion Table

To change	To	Multiply by
ounces (oz.)	grams (g)	28
pounds (lbs.)	kilograms (kg)	0.45
teaspoons	milliliters (ml)	5
tablespoons	milliliters (ml)	15
fluid ounces (fl. oz.)	milliliters (ml)	30
cups	liters (l)	0.24
pints (pt.)	liters (l)	0.47
quarts (qt.)	liters (l)	0.95
gallons (gal.)	liters (l)	3.8
Fahrenheit temperature (°F)	Celsius temperature (°C)	5/9 after subtracting 32